# The American Idea, Resilience, and Thrivancy Education

Dexter Chapin

Series in Education

VERNON PRESS

www.vernonpress.com

*In the Americas:*
Vernon Press
1000 N West Street, Suite 1200
Wilmington, Delaware, 19801
United States

*In the rest of the world:*
Vernon Press
C/Sancti Espiritu 17,
Malaga, 29006
Spain

Series in Education

Library of Congress Control Number: 2024940081

ISBN: 979-8-8819-0126-4

Also available: 978-1-64889-948-5 [Hardback]; 979-8-8819-0071-7 [PDF, E-Book]

# Table of Contents

# List of Figures

# Foreword

## Dr. Barry Clemson
*President, Earth Viability Center*

Listen!

You will hear a huge babel of voices, each proclaiming one or another aspect of the great transition humankind is undergoing ... and many of them are insisting that we face utter ruin unless we make that transition very quickly indeed. I make no pretense of fully understanding this great transition, but I can point to some key aspects. Dexter Chapin's book provides a penetrating analysis of the education we need to make this transition relatively painlessly.

Humankind has undergone several great transitions. First, from hunter-gather tribes to the age of agriculture and nation states. Second, from agriculture to the age of industry and multi-national corporations. Today, we are in the throes of another great transition whose outlines are still emerging. The previous transitions were primarily shifts in the means of securing our food, shelter, and the other necessities of life.

Most of humankind's history has been dominated by scarcity ... getting enough to eat and the material "stuff" for a good life required a lifetime of hard work. Quite suddenly, we are faced with abundance ... our industrial civilization easily produces more than we can use, and the advertising experts are busy creating "needs" to get us to buy all the stuff being manufactured. Even with food there is abundance. For example, the United States throws away 40% of the food it produces ... while millions starve in Africa. We have not yet figured out how to live equitably and sustainably with an industrial civilization committed to always producing more.

The first two great transitions (into agriculture, then into corporate industrialization) certainly changed humankind's image and identity, e.g., from a hunter to a farmer to a laborer. However, industrialization and Newtonian physics enthroned humankind as special and superior and separate from nature. The current transition is more about our psyche ... how we think, what we feel, what stories and foundational myths guide our individual and collective behavior ... in short, our level of consciousness/spirituality is shifting under our feet … and this means we are no longer sure about who/what we are … We must create a new identity for ourselves. Quite obviously, the education we provide for ourselves is a crucial aspect of this transition … which of course explains the frantic efforts of our right wing to ban books and eliminate any aspect of our education that might enlarge student's imaginations or to help them think critically or grow morally.

An early aspect of the current transition involved cybernetics in the 1940s and continued with systems theory, Chaos theory, complexity theory … and we discovered that our common sense and intuitions were often completely wrong. Then, along came quantum physics to upend everything.

Our fundamental ways of thinking and understanding the world have been based on dualism: white or black, my tribe or "others," good or bad, hot or cold, A or not A. In this world, you can't have both A and not A at the same time, you have either one or the other but not both. And here comes quantum physics blithely telling us the world is not like that. We currently have two contradictory theories about how quantum physics works. These theories contradict each other … A and not A. And yet, the engineers are building useful, real-world machines based on both contradictory theories.

Quantum physics is presenting another, possibly even more troubling, idea. It seems that everything might have some level of consciousness. Paired electrons communicate instantaneously across multiple light years of distance. Mycelium networks link the entirety of vast forests and somehow communicate quickly across those distances. Forests are now known to function as one giant organism. The Gaia hypothesis posits that all life on earth collaborates to create the conditions for life to sustain itself. And the biologists are now ensuring us that we humans are utterly dependent on nature … without the multitude of services that nature provides we can't survive.

### The Great Transition

Our old certainties, stories, identities are seen as inadequate or just plain wrong. We are in the midst of a great psychic struggle … everything is in turmoil and Chaos as the old age ends and a new age struggles to be born. Probably the best we can do in defining where we are headed in this great transition is to point to certain key aspects.

Thomas Berry (priest, cultural historian, ecologist) "believed that humanity, after generations spent in despoiling the planet, is poised to embrace a new role as a vital part of a larger, interdependent Earth community, consisting of a 'communion of subjects not a collection of objects'"[1] Berry thought of humankind, nature, and the universe itself as engaged in a cosmic dance of evolution toward more complexity and higher consciousness. Berry's, *The Great Work*,[2] argued that facilitating this evolutionary dance was the critical task for our age.

Perhaps the most fundamental aspect of the current great transition is that humankind seems to be moving to a new level of consciousness/spirituality. Ken Wilber studied almost 200 different developmental schemas. For example, Piaget developed the cognitive developmental schema. Kohlberg devised a moral development schema. A common feature of these schemas is that an individual at one level is unable to understand the thinking/feeling/behavior of someone at the next higher level. A simple example of this is that young children do not have the concept of "conservation of volume." When a toddler is shown water being poured back and forth between a tall thin glass and a short fat glass, they will insist that the volume changes as the water is poured into the taller glass. Similarly, a person at the level of "my family or tribe vs all the others" can't fully grasp the implications of "my tribe is all of humanity." Wilber argues that humankind as-a-whole is in the midst of transitioning to a new (higher) level of consciousness/spirituality. This emerging level of consciousness is a movement toward justice, equality, diversity, and inclusiveness. The rise of right-wing populism, e.g., Donald Trump and his cult, is in large part a backlash against this emerging consciousness in all of its manifestations.

**Aspects of the Great Transition**

The combination of a new consciousness and a civilization of massive complexity is driving us to rethink almost everything. This section briefly touches on the law, government, and the economy, all of which depend upon the sort of education Dexter Chapin's book advocates.

- Commons. Elinor Ostrom's *Governing the Commons*[3] showcases the ancient practices that were rapidly being lost but are now more necessary than ever. Economists "proved" that the commons could not work (Garret Harding's famous "Tragedy of the Commons") but in fact they do work and have been working for centuries. Ostrom's Nobel prize winning work documents how they work and what is required to keep them healthy. As our world shrinks (more people and easier transportation) the commons of land, water, wilderness, air become ever more critical for the well-being of all life and are an increasingly important aspect of the emerging future.

- Legal. Fritjov Capra and Ugo Mattei argue for a new sort of legal system in *The Ecology of Law*[4]. The bedrock concepts for our current legal system are private ownership and state sovereignty. This legal system essentially ignores two arenas that are now critical for our future, i.e., the common good and the critical role of the services nature provides. This legal framework developed during the transition to the industrial age .... a time when the commons were abundant, and the capital needed for industrialization was scarce. This situation is now reversed. Capital is abundant (some would say too abundant in that the very rich are dominating our governments) and the commons are already scarce, and the remaining ones are rapidly being lost to privatization. An ecological legal system rests upon three bedrock principles:

  • Disconnecting law from power and violence and vesting the law in community norms, much like the cultural norms for a viable commons as described by Ostrom.

  • Making community sovereign (instead of the nation state).

  • Making property generative (instead of a source of rent). This shifts property from a source of unearned wealth to serving the common good.

A legal system along these lines empowers communities, the common good, and the rights of nature.

- Economic. The currently dominant economic system, whether described as capitalist or communist, is based on continual growth, unlimited resource extraction, and massive collateral damage, i.e. pollution of land, water, and air and destruction of the Earths life support system. In short, this economic system is rapidly driving civilization towards suicide ... it is now very clear that civilization can't long survive "business as usual." The New Economics Foundation, David Schweickart, and Charles Eisenstein are a few of the voices suggesting new sorts of economies that will be more viable. Solidarity Economy is a loose coalition of folks experimenting with new economic arrangements. Similarly, there is a major movement toward coops of all sorts. Frederic Laloux's, *Reinventing Organizations*,[5] provides case studies of companies that have gotten rid of "bosses" and the hierarchy of authority and power. These companies rely upon empowered workers and work units. Unlike traditional companies bound by the need to maximize profits, these companies consider profit only one among many critical variables, including benefits to their community, workers, and customers. These companies are adaptive, creative, and very profitable. People love working there.

- Government. The cybernetician, Stafford Beer, in *Platform for Change*,[6] argued that many of our institutions were "structurally incompetent." A "Structurally Incompetent" institution has a formal structure that renders it unable to deal with the complexity it is supposedly managing. For example, a general-purpose legislative body such the US congress is expected to create policies and laws. The bills that these officials vote on are often hundreds or thousands of pages long and are the result of much horse-trading among diverse interests, especially the perverse influence of the major corporations and the ultra-rich. These legislators have neither the time nor the expertise to gain a real understanding of the multitude of problem-situations they are expected to legislate about. The inevitable results of this process include:

  - The legislators vote on "sound bites" rather than the actual provisions in the bill.

  - The bills often contain contradictory provisions.

  - In most cases, the bills provide perks to special interests at the expense of the general public.

  - More often than not the bills create more problems than they solve because the dynamic behavior of complex systems is usually counter-intuitive. Thus, here in the USA, we see highly touted governmental initiatives such as the war on terror, war on drugs, or no child left behind … and in all these cases it seems likely that we are worse off than we were before.

Beer argued that we needed to completely rethink our governmental and economic institutions such that they were equipped to deal with massive complexity.

Democracy R&D and the New Democracy Foundation are developing and putting into practice "structurally competent" institutions, i.e., institutional arrangements that do manage extreme complexity and that demonstrate "deliberative democracy" passing laws that effectively promote the common good.

Another key aspect of "structural incompetence" is arbitrary political boundaries. For instance, a medium sized river watershed typically includes hundreds of towns, counties, cities, states and, in many cases, two or more nation states. A river watershed is one of nature's key systems. And a major lesson from all of the various systems sciences is that systems <u>must </u>be dealt with wholistically. Planet Earth's rivers and bioregions are sick and rapidly getting sicker. If we are to avoid destroying the Earth's life support system (and ourselves!), then we have no choice but to manage our river watersheds as systems. This requires major changes in our governmental units.

**An Informed Public**

The US founding fathers were keenly aware of the need for an informed public. Unfortunately, here in the USA we may have the least informed (and most misled) public in our history. Our mass media spent decades presenting "both sides" of every issue as if right-wing disinformation should be given the same consideration as the consensus of the scientists. In recent years even this "both sides" gloss has all but disappeared with the extreme consolidation of both newspapers and television stations into the hands of ultra-rich right-wing owners. Social media has seriously exacerbated this flood of disinformation. Too many of our citizens seem to have lost all ability to think critically about the stories they are being fed and that they endlessly repeat. A robust education is critical if we are ever to have serious discussions about the state of our world and what sort of future we want to work toward.

We in the USA are currently battling over every aspect of education from pre-schools through university. On the surface, there are a great many different issues that are being fought over. The real issue, however, has to do with the great transition: will our education system resist or facilitate the great transition? Dexter Chapin's book describes the educational system required to facilitate humankind's transition to a new level of consciousness and a viable planetary civilization.

**The Planetary Emergency**

Thousands of scientists are warning that we are on the very brink of utter catastrophe from global warming, pollution and too many people for a finite planet. There is substantial literature under the general heading of "Collapsology." I will briefly mention three of the threads in this literature.

- Peak Energy. Thomas Homer-Dixon, *The Upside of Down,*[7] argues that energy shortages have been central in the downfall of every previous civilization. Our current situation is that the return on investment (ROI) for oil has gone from 100 to very near 1 in 153 years. For the first oil wells, using one gallon of oil gained a hundred gallons. We are now getting just slightly more than one gallon for every gallon expended. Clearly, if the ROI goes to one, i.e., it requires a gallon to get a gallon, then there is no point to it. Homer-Dixon argues the age of oil is about over; we are squandering the remaining oil to, e.g. make plastics that we could do without, and that the transition to alternate fuels is unlikely to be possible in time to avoid a collapse.

- Elites. Margaret Wheatley's *Who do We Choose to be*[8], reviews the literature on the collapse of civilizations and concludes that our global civilization is in serious trouble because our elites are corrupt. Throughout history, the elites in new civilizations start out with a strong commitment to public service and the common good. Over a period of roughly ten generations, the elites gradually lose their commitment to service and become self-serving, greedy, and corrupt. We have no example of a civilization recovering after its elites become corrupt. Our current situation is unique in that there are no barbarians next door to replace our civilization ... the current civilization is world-wide, and it is all we have. Wheatley argues that our elites are very corrupt, that civilization will collapse and that we need to create islands of sanity that could persist even in the midst of this collapse.

- Convergence of Crises. Pablo Servigne and Raphael Stevens, *How Everything Can Collapse*,[9] discuss the multiple crises converging on us all at once. While our institutions may be able to handle major crises, none of them are able to handle multiple simultaneous crises. "Failed states" are nations in which the central government is unable to exert control over and provide basic service to the major regions of the country. There are currently 26 failed or nearly failed states. In the USA, the polarization among the general population and the failure of Congress to develop any meaningful legislation during 2023 do not inspire confidence.

In conclusion, we have very strong scientific evidence that 1) we are in a dire planetary emergency and 2) there is very little time to avoid the collapse of civilization, wide-spread famines and deaths, and a reversion to much degraded technological base for the survivors.

### Culture, Stories and Education

Every human culture has always been shaped and directed by its stories and foundational myths. Two of the key stories of our current age are:

- The story of "More"... the good life depends on more money, more stuff, more fame, etc.

- The myth of continual growth … the economy must grow; production and consumption must grow without end.

The story that "more "leads to happiness and fulfillment directs much of our behavior … even though most of us know this doesn't work.

The myth of continual growth ignores the very inconvenient fact that it is clearly impossible. To quote the eminent economist and polymath, Kenneth Boulding "Anyone who believes exponential growth can go on forever in a finite world is either a madman or an economist."

## The Birth of New Stories

Cybernetics and the more recent systems sciences have demonstrated that our world is more a creation of our own minds than previously understood. Heinz von Foerster put it this way "The opposite of objectivity is responsibility." These new sciences also demonstrated that systems abound … everywhere, at all scales from the sub-atomic to the universe itself, we find systems which behave as entities. Further, within systems the relationships among the parts are more important than the parts themselves.

Buckminster Fuller jogged our collective imaginations with his "Spaceship Earth" image. Suddenly we are confronted with the idea of earth as a finite system (a ship) traveling through space. This implies that we had best learn to be good stewards of our ship. Pictures of earth taken from space further enlarged our imaginations.

Lovelock and Margulis took this a step further with the Gaian paradigm shift[10] which argues that the entirety of the Earth's biosphere constituted a system that created and maintained the conditions that it needs to thrive. An obvious corollary is that if we disturb Gaia too much, it will eventually cause this planetary system to shift into some entirely new state … and this new state may or may not be hospitable for humans.

Physics is often considered the queen of the sciences and, as such, has always been important in shaping our conceptions of ourselves and the universe. As mentioned above, quantum physics is upending both our image of ourselves and of the universe. *The Dancing Wu Li Masters*,[11] a book on quantum physics based on conversations between physicists and Buddhist monks, says "no one understands quantum physics." Perhaps meditation and Zen are as useful in understanding quantum physics as are experiments and data.

David Korten wrote about this in *Change the Story, Change the Future*.[12] Charles Eisenstein hosts a web forum aptly called "The new and Ancient Story" with more than 4 thousand participants[13]. Joe Brewer, also with more than four thousand participants, is working on how we might manage the evolution of our cultures and the regeneration of our bioregions.[14]

To paraphrase Martin Luther King, the moral arc of the universe bends toward justice. This can mean nothing else except that all the great battles for justice and equality are truly one battle. The age of old white European patriarchy is over. We are seeing the birth pangs of a new age of justice, equality, diversity, and inclusiveness.

I don't know what the new stories will be. However, I am certain the new stories undergirding the Great Transition will emphasize love for all life, including reverence for nature.

It is very hard to see how we can possibly manage this Great Transition without Thrivancy Education.

### References

[1] "Thomas Berry," Wikipedia, accessed January 19, 2024, https://en.wikipedia.org/wiki/Thomas_Berry.

[2] Thomas Berry, *The Great Work: Our Way into the Future*, (New York: Crown, 2013).

[3] Elinor Ostrom, *Governing the Commons: The Evolution of Institutions for Collective Action*, (Cambridge: Cambridge University Press, 1990).

[4] Fritjof Capra, and Ugo Mattei, *The Ecology of Law*, (Berrett-Koehler Publishers, 2015).

[5] Frederic Laloux, *Reinventing Organizations: A Guide to Creating Organizations Inspired by the next Stage of Human Consciousness*, (Brussels: Nelson Parker, 2014).

[6] Stafford Beer, *Platform for Change*, (John Wiley & Sons, 2000).

[7] Thomas Homer-Dixon, *The Upside of Down*, (Island Press, 2010).

[8] Margaret J. Wheatley, *Who Do We Choose to Be? Facing Reality, Claiming Leadership, Restoring Sanity*, (Oakland: Berrett-Koehler Publishers, 2017).

[9] Pablo Servigne, Raphael Stevens, and Andrew Brown, *How Everything Can Collapse: A Manual for Our Times*, (Cambridge, UK: Polity, 2020).

[10] James E. Lovelock, *Gaia a New Look at Life on Earth*, (Oxford, UK: Oxford University Press, 1979).

[11] Gary Zukav, *The Dancing Wu Li Masters*, (Harper Collins, 2009).

[12] David C. Korten, *Change the Story, Change the Future: A Living Economy for a Living Earth: A Report to the Club of Rome*, (Oakland, California: Berrett-Koehler, 2015).

[13] Charles Eisenstein, "A New and Ancient Story Network," https://www.naascommunity.org, accessed March 10, 2024.

[14] Joe Brewer, "Design School for Regenerating Earth," https://design-school-for-regenerating-earth.mn.co/, accessed March 30, 2024.

# Preface

I did not plan to become a teacher, but through happenstance fell into the only job I might be good at. I loved teaching and am proud to have been a teacher, but that is not the point. Schools give teachers the opportunity, if they choose, to sit in one of the best possible grandstand seats to observe what is happening in their community and beyond. They have a raft of reporters arriving every day, ready to tell their story as they come through the door. Not always in words, not always in actions, sometimes in silence, and sometimes in tragedies.

Students have the capacity to point out the blind spots, the unseen, unheard, and ignored. I spent over half a century in K-12 education being educated by kids. It's not always students. Parents, administrators, occasionally police or a judge, and often other teachers, coaches and staff deliver the news. You watch, you listen, you ask a question every now and then, and you see, you learn, and sometimes you understand, and sometimes you respond.

This book is a response. I treasured my place in the grandstand, made possible by my teachers, my mentors, and my coaches. This book is a precis of all that I learned from my kids, the adults, and my experience.

This is not intended as an academic treatise. The references are almost all readily available, popular sources if the reader wishes to explore farther. The older, referenced books are generally available in digital formats. I have taken what is commonly known and woven it into a new pattern that generates hope that we can regain the ability to thrive.

I expect my readers to be those people who look out the window and wonder why America seems to be moving backwards? How did we elect the people we elected? Why are we banning books? Why are we losing ground financially, socially, and spiritually? It is too easy to call something fascist, and I never do, but the expression used to be, "The clouds of Fascism are always on the horizon in America, but it rains in Europe." These days, the rain squalls are coming closer. They are just one town, or one state, over. How is this happening in America and what can we do about it? This book provides an answer to those questions.

# Acknowledgements

The writing has taken years. Every time I say I am done, the reporters say, "No, you're not." I must thank the teachers, mentors, and coaches with whom I shared schools. Equally, there were the shipmates, mechanics, best friends, and those I just brushed up against in life. Some are gone, but I still listen to them. The members of The Freedom Road Global Writers Group will all see their work here. Of the students, some have stuck around for decades. They never stop teaching.

Every one of them worked at helping me see the beauty hidden from me because I did not try enough to understand. The major credit goes to Karen. Without her beside me, through thick and thin, here and there, with and without, this book would not exist, and neither would I. I Love you.

Chapter 1

# Introduction

Suppose one morning, you wake up in a dystopian country. A country where you had to have a government license to write a blog or a podcast about the government. A place where children designated to be on the "McDonalds Track" would not take Algebra. Where children would only have government approved books to read and could carry weapons of war down the sidewalk. Where it would be a crime to vaccinate children. Where vigilantes would be rewarded for preventing you from travelling. Where it would be alright for police to open your mail without a warrant. A country lacking any sort of safety net for the old, the sick, or the incapacitated. And a country, a playground for the elite, where the top 1% controlled almost three quarters of privately held wealth, essentially obligation and tax free.

This is not an accurate portrayal of America. At least, not yet, but everything and more described in that paragraph has been, and is being, proposed. There is huge pressure to move towards that dystopian, repressive future, and too many of us are asleep at the wheel. We are on a path to trouble. To put it bluntly, we are approaching a crisis. We find it harder and harder to agree on much of anything. Common ground is disappearing, and there is less and less room for a solid, shared foundation of ideas, beliefs, and norms that allows a community to grow, succeed, and thrive. The American Idea and its product, the American middle class, is under greater threat than it ever has been during our lives.

As in all complex, long-running stories, there are two sides to today's American story. At this point in time, those challenging the American Idea seem to have the upper hand. But there is a hero just stepping into the story and changing the plot. In this story, Gen Z is identified as the hero, and a way to support and strengthen their impact is formulated.

This is a story that starts where we are today, and how we got here. From the earliest declarations, America has been a country based on a broadly shared ethos, or idea, of equality, justice, freedom, and self-determination. An ethos is shared but not always agreed to in detail or meaning. Even with the variances and disagreements, the American Idea expressed a broadly shared pattern or paradigm.

A paradigm is a shared code including a set of rules, definitions, assumptions, concepts, values, practices, and connections that allow one to assign meaning, or not, to a constant flow of inputs, stimuli, and experiences. A shared paradigm is a shared understanding of a pattern. A pattern and a paradigm are different. A pattern exists. A paradigm may be developed to describe an existing pattern, such as General Systems Theory or Newtonian Mechanics, or to create a pattern where none exists, such as Morse Code.

The term paradigm is used here instead of pattern to differentiate how complicated, nuanced, multi-layered, and complex these sorts of paradigms tend to be. All paradigms are limited. No paradigm can provide all the answers all the time. That would be an ideology. Positive paradigms may devolve over time into destructive ideologies.

In 1853, the abolitionist minister, Theodore Parker, suggested that the moral arc of the Universe could be bent towards justice if people worked at it. The beliefs and meanings associated with the American Idea have shaped history as they have been bent in the direction of Justice, usually at the cost of blood, pain, death, and mourning. However, Martin Luther King still had confidence that the statement was true in 1968.

In 1997, Strauss and Howe wrote,

> History is seasonal, and winter is coming. The very survival of the nation will feel at stake. Sometime before the year 2025, America will pass through a great gate in history, commensurate with the American Revolution, Civil War, and the twin emergencies of the Great Depression in World War II. The risk of catastrophe will be high. The nation could erupt into insurrection or civil violence, crack up geographically or succumb to authoritarian rule. If there is a war, it is likely to be one of maximum risk and effort – in other words, a total war. Every Fourth Turning has registered an upward ratchet in the technology of destruction, and in mankind's willingness to use it. [1, p.6]

> This book takes no position on Strauss and Howe's approach to understanding History. The focus here is on the predictions they made in the 1990s about the present.

Strauss and Howe suggested that America would enter a crisis stage sometime in the middle 2010s. The economic collapse of 2008 is as close as you can get, and we have been spiraling in towards a full-blown crisis ever since.

Strauss and Howe suggest the crisis will be a war of some sort. As we have gone through the elections of 2020 and 2022, it seems that maybe we are entering a crisis of confidence, trust, and identity. All three of which are about a lack of Resilience.

The American Idea and the arc towards Justice are threatened by a network of government and nongovernmental actors at the nexus of which is the far right wing of the Republican Party.

> The terms "Republican" and "Republican Party" almost always refer not to your parents' party, but to a new party formed in the image of the previous President.

A large segment of the party has eschewed the concept of an explicit platform or identity in favor of doing the bidding of oligarchs, some of whom have supported a goal of destroying democracy and the present status quo.

The net result is the onslaught of well-funded mediocrities such as Blake Masters, J.D. Vance, Margaret Taylor Greene, and Lauren Boebert. To say these individuals wish to protect and enhance equality, justice, freedom, and self-determination is to fly in the face of reality. They are too busy suggesting life-saving medicine is satanic, looking for space lasers, and suggesting women are "lesser vessels."

> Peter Thiel, "Since 1920, the vast increase in welfare beneficiaries and the extension of the franchise to women — two constituencies that are notoriously tough for libertarians — have rendered the notion of 'capitalist democracy' into an oxymoron."[8]

Twenty-five years ago, Strauss and Howe predicted the rise of the militias such as the Proud Boys, the Patriot Front, the Aryan Nation, and the Oath Keepers. These may be the headliners, but the Constitutional Sheriffs are rapidly and quietly growing as trust in the larger social organization breaks down. Every one of these groups is anti-democracy, white supremacist, and deeply enfolded into the far right-wing of American politics. Every one of these groups fulfills the prophecy.

> Powerful new civic organizations will make judgments about which individual rights deserve respect and which do not. Criminal justice will become swift and rough, trampling on some innocents to protect an endangered and desperate society from those feared to be guilty. Vagrants will be rounded up, the mentally ill recommitted, criminal appeals short-circuited, executions hastened. [1, p.276]

Within the State and Federal governments, the Supreme Court is working diligently to give states permission to limit or rescind what have been constitutional rights. Money as speech, gerrymandering, and limited voting access have direct and potentially lethal impacts on the American Idea of equality, justice, freedom, and self-determination.

As Strauss and Howe predicted, the mediocrities, on the Supreme Court, Alito, Thomas, Kavanaugh, Gorsuch, Roberts, and Comey, are all the illegitimate politicians in robes, products of the Federalist Society, broken norms, outright perjury, and the buying and selling of justice by the friends of Leonard Leo.[9]

The danger to the American Idea is not found just at the federal level. The threat occurs at every level from school boards to the state legislatures. Volumes could be written about the thousands of efforts being made to limit what can be taught in school, and to limit who can vote.

Teachers and school districts can be fined for teaching about the realities of American chattel slavery because it might cause students some embarrassment. In the recent Arizona election, if you wanted to vote early and place your ballot in a drop box, you might have come face-to-face with masked, armed, white, thugs challenging your actions.[10]

Much of the effort to move America in a repressive direction is supported by individual oligarchs, some of whom you have heard about such as the Koch brothers, Peter Thiel, Robert Mercer, Robert Murdoch, Leonard Leo, the DeVos family, and perhaps most ostentatiously, Elon Musk. Others are less well known, such as the right-wing branch of the Uihlein family, and many take us by surprise when they donate huge amounts of money to bankroll the party with tens, sometimes hundreds, of millions of dollars.

These oligarchs consider themselves the best, the brightest, and the independent, self-willed, movers and shakers. It might shock them to know their performance was predicted decades ago as a part of a "high-tech oligarchy."[1] It might displease them even more to understand that they are a fading influence of relatively short-term importance as they ravage the decaying carcass of the state.[2]

Strauss and Howe predicted that at the end of the 2025's crisis, a new generation of heroes would arise. Their expectation was that it would be those labelled Millennials. And certainly, the Millennials have been carrying the "youth" or "younger" designation for a while. However, based on their performance to date, it seems the new hero generation burst onto the scene with the mid-term elections, Generation Z.

There was a good deal of 2022 election anxiety. The pre-election polls suggested a red wave. It was feared that the American Idea was about to take a serious body blow. Hundreds of Republican candidates were election deniers[3] and would not, or could not, state they would accept any outcome but victory.

To quote an old cliché, "Prediction is very difficult, especially if it is about the Future." The red wave did not happen. If 2022 was when Strauss and Howe's fourth turning was possible, the crisis event was delayed. A good thing, because while the fourth turning predicts a change, it does not predict towards the light or the dark. Steve Bannon, a reputed fan of Strauss and Howe, and a chief strategist for the former President, had worked hard, as had many others, to make sure the wave would sweep us towards the dark.

The wave did not materialize. The mediocrities and the deniers who were victorious were in hard red areas where any Republican would have a very difficult time losing, and even then, some, e.g., Lauren Boebert, came very close to losing. Elsewhere, the deniers lost. Kari Lake, Arizona's Republican governor candidate and vociferous denier, refused to accept her loss and flew to Mar-a-Lago to commiserate with the biggest denier of all. She called for a massive demonstration. Fifteen people showed up.

> A typical Gen Zer is a self-driver who deeply cares about others, strives for a diverse community, is highly collaborative and social, values flexibility, relevance, authenticity, non-hierarchical leadership, and, while dismayed about inherited issues like climate change, has a pragmatic attitude about the work that has must be done to address those issues.[4]

The fact that the red wave did not happen is directly attributable to the arrival of Gen Z; also known as the Zoomers, Centennials, *i*Generation, or Homelanders. The defining element of Gen Z that sets them apart is their racial, gendered, economic, geographic, and spiritual diversity. Whatever name you might call them, they showed up, they voted, and they changed the outcomes.

Gen Z's diversity short-circuited the catastrophe, but the crisis is not over. If the American Idea is to survive, Gen Z needs to keep showing up. There will be a crescendo of mini-crises between the midterms and the election aftermaths of 2024. There will be indictments. There will be trials and possibly convictions with sentences to be served. Each of these is new, uncharted territory, with unknown terrain and unpredictable dangers.

Short of a cataclysmic event, the unknowns and unpredictable can be navigated without a full-blown crisis. The real battle and crisis generator will be the 2024 election. But Gen Z needs allies to help fight the battles that may be generated before, during, and after that election. This is not a prediction of a new "civil war." This is a prediction that no matter what happens at the Federal level, some individual states will continue to limit and dim the American Idea.

This book is about creating opportunities for those allies to develop across the states. We must counteract a denial of history, the simplification of the present, a loss of connection, the breakdown of community, the loss of opportunity, and the denial of justice and equity by the dominant cultural ideology.

Gen Z provides us with a model solution for the present misfeasance and malfeasance threatening the American Idea. We will build on that model in some detail. In doing so, we move across history, social systems, and social structures. However, while showing the direction to go, there is no precise step-by-step path. Precisely because the American Idea defies precision, there can be no precise recipe, model, or commandments for solutions.

However, at the core of any response is the concept of Resilience. The defense of the American Idea demands three steps: making cultural Resilience a priority, learning how to create and grow resiliency, and rebuilding the social systems to do so.

Three simple steps and the issue is done. The steps may sound simple. They will not be easy. Resiliency is an inherent threat to the status quo. We already know how to create Resiliency in children; we just stopped doing so. We already have the systems in place. We just stopped using them. We need to start threatening the status quo by restarting the systems to create resilient children. Every success in doing so will be similar, but every success must be local. Societal success will be multiple instances, with multiple approaches, addressing multiple panoramas.

The 2022 midterms are history, but the dangers and threat remain. If Gen Z, and allies up and down the age groupings, cannot prevent the rebirth of a crisis in 2024, what sort of future story will we tell about what happened to the American Idea? Will it be the same sort of story as the Titanic, or the Hindenburg, or the Miracle on the Hudson?

The Titanic was the biggest, the best, the most beautiful, and coveted, ship in the World, but on April 15th, 1912 in the cold, dark, North Atlantic, the Titanic sank, killing over two thirds of the people on board.

A small coal-bunker fire had been discovered as the ship departed Southampton. In and of itself, the fire would play no role in the proceedings.

But it is always possible for a fire to grow unseen, and a fearful captain might feel the best path forward would be faster, straighter, and with no deviations.

The Titanic captain had hours of warnings about the icefield, but he was looking at the World through a paradigm, in part perhaps, built of fear and could only see fast, and straight, and with no deviations. He knew no alternatives. His paradigm had become an ideology and over fifteen hundred people died cold, lonely deaths.

In the last twenty years, there have been increasing social or cultural bunker-fires, including increased vigilantism by police, increasing actual and threatened violence to support socio-cultural bullying, and a dramatic increase in random mass murders. If we add in the decimation of Main Street in 2008 and the dislocations due to climate change, and the aftermath of COVID-19, it is very clear we are headed into icefields, physically, socially, economically, and culturally. "Majorities of Americans say they feel 'fearful' (62%) and 'angry' (55%) when thinking about the state of the country."[6]

Those whom we called, "Captains of Industry" but now, more accurately, call "oligarchs," are demanding a response of faster, straighter, and no deviations. There are a few other oligarch voices, but the choir is almost unanimous, and amplified by the right-wing of the Republican Party. This time, not thousands, but, locally and globally, tens of millions are potentially going to die.

The Titanic story metaphorically gives us time to change course. A second possible story about the death of the American Idea doesn't give us that luxury. On May 6th, 1937, the airship Hindenburg caught fire and was destroyed in less than a minute. Where the Titanic captain could not see alternatives, the captain of the Hindenburg did see alternatives and acted on them. The story of the Hindenburg is a story of decisions made, and actions taken, with unexpected and unintended consequences.

As the Hindenburg was approaching the Lakehurst mooring tower, in deteriorating weather, the captain altered his normal approach to a path requiring a sharp left turn quickly followed by a right turn. It is postulated the stress of the turns caused an interior reinforcing cable to break, puncturing one of the hydrogen cells, allowing hydrogen to be ignited by a spark of uncertain origin that brought the airship down in about 37 seconds.[11]

If one is looking at the World through a tunnel, the possibilities of unintended consequences are often invisible, but the realities are not. The Hindenburg is a case where the paradigm

> The purpose of the system, any system, is what it does. The purposes of The Supreme Court's radical revisioning are precisely outcomes of disenfranchisement, deaths, and control of the many by the few.

was incomplete and could not deal with the unknown complexity. Over the last two decades, the Supreme Court has radically redirected our political and social path in terms of free speech, voting rights, personal privacy, and protection from industrial harm. When combined with policies fomenting economic and social inequities, the stage is set for something to break. It is unknown where the spark might originate but, in this story, the death of the American Idea may well be unexpected, explosive, and rapid.

However, all is not lost. There is yet a potential third sort of story, the story of the Miracle on the Hudson. On January 15, 2009, U.S. Airways Flight 1549 started on a flight from La Guardia to North Carolina that lasted about 5 minutes and ended on the Hudson River. At about three minutes into the flight, both engines swallowed Canada geese and stopped working. Captain Chesley Sullenberger was cleared to return to La Guardia. He determined that was not going to work. He was cleared to Teterboro Airport and agreed, but thought it through, and chose instead to land on the Hudson River.

He landed the plane at 140 mph close to the river ferries. They were the only nearby boats large enough to hold the 155 people on the plane, four with injuries and one serious injury, needing quick rescue with the air at 19 degrees and the river at 41. While the ferries were crucial, the landing site was immediately swarming with federal, state, city, and private boats, all playing a role. Nobody died.[12]

This is a very different story from the first two. First, if Captain Sullenberger was looking at the World through a tunnel, he might have chosen Teterboro. After all, planes are supposed to land at airports. Instead, he worked through three alternatives, chose one and recruited assistance from multiple sources on the ground and on the plane to increase chances of success. He directed

> A crucial point here is that everybody exercised choice. The pilot, the crew, the passengers, and the responders all controlled a range of choices. They chose to do this rather than that.

the play, but it was not a solo act. Everybody involved, especially the passengers, refused to panic, acted with courage, and focused on making the situation better. It is worth repeating, everybody survived to live another day. They even got their luggage back.

If the American Idea is the vehicle to get us to another place we want to be, and it suddenly suffers a catastrophe, it does not have to end badly. It is possible, with quick thinking, action without panic, and a great deal of involvement and heavy lifting by the community, to end well. This is a description, almost a definition, of thriving in the face of change.

But what does it mean to thrive? Does it mean everybody is rich, has a new car, lives in a nice house, has a boss who totally appreciates them, and has a placid existence. Yes, it does mean that, and no, that is a totally inadequate description.

To thrive, in the most general terms, means to lead a life of social, emotional, and psychological well-being. The social facet is about having a network of connections with others, near and far, who listen, support, and challenge.[13] The emotional facet is about having confidence in an optimistic explanatory perspective about difficulty and change. The psychological facet is about experiential and action-based self-knowledge, self-confidence, and mindfulness.

But there is a fourth facet that is crucial to being able to thrive. You do not thrive if you are simply flotsam and jetsam on the tides of time. There are clearly uncontrolled and uncontrollable elements in everybody's life, but if you go through life bouncing from one hard place to another with random interludes between, you are not thriving. You are surviving. Thriving requires a sense of control in choosing the best course forward and making the best of the life you are dealt.

If you are missing any one of the four facets, you are not really thriving. You may be rich, have a new car, live in a nice house, have a boss who totally appreciates you, and you may have a placid existence. A well-lived life is not a featureless, placid, difficulty or challenge-free, existence. A well-lived life is open to connections with a supportive community that challenges, teaches, and validates a positive, reality-based, perspective about the World and the self. But even that is not thriving if there is an absence of control. Being able to choose an action, a direction of growth, or to select a change in behavior, perspective or belief is a crucial and necessary condition for Thriving.

> The sense of agency refers to the capacity of individuals to act independently and shape their life circumstances. By exerting free will, the person expands his options and freedom. When feeling free and self-determined, we generally flourish.[6]

The exercise of control is the hallmark of Resilience where Resilience is defined as being able to maintain your identity and function in the face of change. Resilience is a product of the other three facets of a well-lived life: the social, the emotional, and the psychological, with the addition of choice. They are mutually causal. Without choice, the other three facets cannot be maintained. They will become less developed, weaker, and Resilience will wither in the face of change.

Resilience allows you to maintain effective membership in social networks by absorbing the daily vagaries of contents and behaviors of network members. A rigid, unchanging set of expectations may maintain connections with the few but, over time, the many will no longer listen, support, or challenge.

Emotional well-being requires the ability to absorb "the slings and arrows of outrageous fortune" without responding, as Hamlet does, with despair. Resilience does not preclude pain and agony. It does allow us to absorb, work around, and move on with acceptance if not joy, and equanimity.

The psychological dimension of well-being is based on the on-going creation of the self through interactions with the social network and the mindfulness that allows development of self-knowledge and confidence based on action.[14] To modify the cliché, Resilience is precisely not doing the same thing over and over again, expecting a different result. Resilience is learning, and changing, and learning again.

This then is the basis for thriving and it is becoming increasingly obvious that large segments of America are not thriving. The following statements hit three aspects of today's cultural fabric as described by Howe.[7p226]

-   Social networks at the individual, community, state, and national levels are being ripped apart such that we are creating islands in a sea of isolation. Bridge building, connecting, and sharing, between islands is so difficult as to be essentially forbidden.[15]

-   Emotional well-being is down. Suicide rates have been climbing for two decades. Increased isolation, loss, and awareness of social inequities, anxiety, and fear are troubling the lives of many.[16]

-   The psychological aspect of thriving is challenged by increased rupturing of community connections with an increase in isolation and a redefinition of self in the face of dwindling community, and emotional support to face a lack of resources and opportunity.[17]

The lack of Resilience is an obvious issue. Many people are just trying to keep on doing what they have been doing, and it is not working. They are not getting the results they expected or hoped for. These insufficient results contribute to anxiety and the questioning of identity and social position; almost the definition of not being resilient.

The lack of American cultural Resilience did not develop overnight. The roots of the issue go back to the late 1950's. Nobody has ever set a goal to reduce our cultural and individual Resilience. It is an unforeseen outcome of decisions made over a period of decades on the individual, social, and political levels. The rate of loss has increased dramatically over the last twenty or so years, partially through bad luck and partially through political malfeasance.

Chapter 2

# How Did We Get Here?

With the enormous advantages that we had coming into the millennium, the question becomes, how did we get here? The short answer is that America has failed to maintain the social and cultural Resilience required to successfully address and adapt to rapidly increasing rates of cultural and social change driven by public health, climate, technology, and societal norms.

Perhaps the most publicly acclaimed driver of change is the COVID-19 pandemic. We have talked about little else for three years. As this is written, the virus has killed over a million of our fellow citizens, and the pandemic has shortened our life span.[15] Further, consider how many hundreds of thousands of children have lost one or two primary caregivers. Those losses have created and are creating a cascade of changes and reverberations throughout the social fabric, each of which is manifested in the lives of individuals. That is a level of failure and change that did not have to happen.

We were warned this was coming. While the specifics were unknown in advance, we knew that over time a pandemic was likely. As part of a desire to erase the previous administration, the Trump administration's response was to defund the expertise and put amateurs in charge. In part, we failed because of the personality of our forty-fifth President. In part, we failed because of our congressional and state leaders. In part, we failed because a long time ago, another President suggested in word and action that, "Greed is good." And, in part, we failed because a dominant cultural paradigm became a set of blinders, precluding effective responses and demanding faster, straighter, with no deviations.

As in the Titanic story, faster, straighter, and no deviations took time to have an impact, but after a delay, those decisions caused death and disruption. Even a short listing gives some feeling for the COVID-19 induced scope of change, and dislocation of our lives.

> The impact has been global. Those without our advantages have starved and died at catastrophic rates. We chose to fail politically and socially. Others had much less choice.

## Work
- Upended normally stable livelihoods, expectations, and careers.
- Working from home changed family dynamics and patterns.
- Created a shift in power dynamics between bosses and workers.

## Education
- Online universities reduced student activities and opportunities away from home.
- Serious reduction in on-the-job training and internships.
- Online learning in K-12 meant less face-to-face coaching, increased truancy, and less richness.

## Home and family
- Generational isolation from those in nursing homes even as they died changed social dynamics, and the grieving process.
- Somewhere above 240,000 children lost a primary or secondary care giver.[16]
- Both parents and children working from home redefined the structure of the house and challenged familial dynamics.

## Medicine, stress, and depression
- Layoffs lead to stress and a degree of loss of personal identity.
- Increased inequities in all the above points had different effects on morale, medical access, and mental health depending on gender, socio-economic status, and race.[15]

## Culture traits
- Racial, socio-economic, gender, geographic, political, and spiritual differences, tensions, and aggressions surfaced and sometimes boiled over at all levels of society. but especially at the local level of town councils and school boards.[17]
- With over 105 million cases of COVID-19, this listing just barely skims the individual, institutional, social, and cultural changes brought about by the pandemic. Every individual, even those who were never sick, will have their own stories to tell of disruption, isolation, depression, and, perhaps, anger about the new normal.

For a while, the pandemic got all the headlines, but there are at least four other sources of change and dislocation having a significant effect: climate change; the rapid growth of "in-your-face" technology, the increase of lying for profit, and the rise of white supremacy / nationalism.

Climate change is already here. During 2021, the total cost of weather and climate disaster events in the U.S. was $145.0 billion.[14] These events were primarily hurricanes, tornadoes, floods, droughts, and hot or cold temperature extremes, with the costs spread in variable amounts across all fifty states. Each of those $145 billion represents a disruption and change, a lost life, house, livelihood, opportunity, or dream.

> In 2020, it was estimated that 1.2 million Americans became climate refugees fleeing storms, droughts, fires, and heat.[1]

We used to talk about the weather. Now we ask rhetorical questions, how many storms will shred the Gulf Coast this year? Can you buy house insurance in Florida? In California? How many 110+ degree days will Phoenix have this year? Will there ever be an end to the drought in the Southwest?

The West Coast from the Pacific, inland to the Rockies, from southern Montana to Mexico, has a history of recurring megadroughts. However, the present Southwest drought is the worst for the last 1200 years with approximately 42 percent of the impact attributable to climate change.[2] The population growth in the Southwest over the last fifty or sixty years has been at least double and sometimes triple the overall growth rate of the country.[18]

The whole area is water short, but Arizona, as the most recent, junior partner, is the first to have its Colorado River allocation reduced. The question of what this means is just beginning to be recognized in Arizona conversations. Four or five years ago, people were talking about water at conferences and in offices but not around swimming pools. That is changing slowly but it is getting real rapidly. Between the drought and reduced river share, some communities are simply out of water. The wells are dry, and neighboring communities are unwilling to share.

Approximately 74% of Arizona's water goes to agriculture.[19] Some of it is allocated to thirsty crops such as cotton, corn, and alfalfa. Some communities are buying water rights from agricultural areas, putting the water into a canal system, bringing it to town to percolate into the local aquifers. These are most likely the opening salvos in the coming water wars. It is too soon to predict the how all this will play out, but an increasing water shortage, combined with an increasing temperature will absolutely and fundamentally change the culture and the viability of the Southwest. Perhaps generating several million more climate change refugees.

Arizona may be a poster child for climate change impacts, but those changes are happening across the continent and in all fifty states. California, Alaska, and Hawaii are burning. The northern tier of states is subject to record breaking heat waves, increased heavy precipitation events with less snow and increased humidity stress. The mid-Atlantic area is looking at increased heavy precipitation with concurrent flooding. The Gulf Coast is being swept away. Florida is slowly becoming Atlantis.[20]

These very generic descriptions smooth over the millions of life-plans changed, expectations dashed, and personal tragedies survived, or not. These are community and state-wide changes that are happening more and more frequently. But many of those in power are Captains of the Titanic demanding faster, straighter, with no deviations.[21]

The Titanic had a course to follow and an objective to arrive at. Technology is a dramatic driver of increasing rates of change without a particular course or objective. It is happening because it can.[3]

In the 1940s, it was suggested that we doubled our knowledge base in 25 years. In 2013, it was estimated that, on average, across disciplines, we doubled our knowledge base every 12-13 months. Recently, IBM suggested that with the development of the internet of things, our knowledge base will double every 12 hours.[4]

> The growth of knowledge is spotty. The internet of things doesn't alter the horizons on the Roman Empire. Part of what we learn is not information. It is a difference that does not make a difference.

In 1966, Marshal McLuhan wrote;

> Today, the ordinary child lives in an electronic environment. He lives in a world of information overload. From infancy, he is confronted with the television image... Any moment of television provides more data than could be recorded in a dozen pages of prose. The next moment provides more pages of prose. The children, so accustomed to a "Niagara of data" in their ordinary environments, are introduced to nineteenth-century classrooms and curricula, where data flow is not only small in quantity but fragmented in pattern. The subjects are unrelated. The environmental clash can nullify motivation in learning.[5]

McLuhan wrote that statement,

when a student's 'connectivity' was limited to passive reception of radio, television, and the printed page. In addition, a student might have a participatory connection via a landline phone, face-to-face conversations, and, again, the printed page. If the data flow was a 'Niagara' in 1966, how would you describe it these days with hundreds of on-demand cable channels, broadband links, ubiquitous wi-fi, multitasking cell phones, and iPods?[6]

We will need to accept the growing complexity and the less ordered nature of things as the World and what we know about it, becomes ever more complicated and unpredictable. Our children are facing a data-driven future the likes of which we have never seen. "70% of today's students will end up in jobs that have not yet been invented. They will collaborate with people on multiple continents through institutions not yet created, struggling to solve problems we do not yet recognize."[7] "The massive shifts technology and globalization that are expected to transform the workplace have already begun. In many industries and countries, some of the most in-demand jobs didn't even exist five or 10 years ago — and the pace of change will only accelerate."[8]

Technology, in general, is a massive driver of change across a broad swath of American Culture. Socially, at a more individual, personal level, the part of technology driving change might be termed the "in-your-face" technology of connectivity via the internet. Prime examples are Facebook and Twitter before Musk. In-your-face technology and the increase of lying for dollars have accelerated the rate of change in the American social structure.

Ronald Reagan was elected president in 1980. By 1988, the marginal tax rate for the highest earners was reduced from 90% during the Eisenhower years and 70% during the sixties and seventies to 28%, with multiple work arounds that reduced the rate further. In addition, it was during this period that the process of phasing out the estate taxes was started. Rather than discouraging excess wealth, Reagan essentially encouraged the rich to be greedy. Greed went from being a moral sin to a policy goal.[9]

The net result was the incentivizing accrual rather than production. The individual's role, function, or production were no longer valued. Their value became their bank account. Magazines were dedicated to listing the 400 wealthiest Americans. Nobody paid a great deal of attention to how the dollars were earned. The total accrual was, and is, important.

It is a straight line from there to Fox News in general, Tucker Carlson, and to lesser lights such as Alex Jones. All of whom lie for profit. Fox News and Tucker are mega-corporations and do not need Facebook, but Facebook is a wonderful

> The Dominion lawsuit made public that Murdoch, and Carlson, among many others, recognized and discussed that telling the truth was toxic for their business plan.

megaphone for the small-business liar. Both big and small liars have precisely the same business model, the bigger the lie, the bigger the profit.

The profits can be egregious, but the subsidies are death, disruption, anger, violence, and the general fraying of the social fabric. Facts may be unpalatable. Truth might be hard to accept, but lies are poisonous, and destroy the ability to thrive.

In America, Tucker Carlson has been a loud voice transforming white supremacy into white nationalism by the addition of fear. A fear described by Howard Thurman as "like the fog in San Francisco or in London. It is nowhere in particular yet everywhere."[10] The people who live in this fog know the World is changing around them. They know that tomorrow is going to be different, but they are not sure how. They feel that others are doing better. Others know and understand. Others are taking advantage, getting ahead. They are being left behind, but they don't know why, or how. They are powerless to respond.

This fear grows best in the dark, fed a diet of horse manure. In this case, the horses include Tucker Carlson, the former president, Joe Rogan, Franklin Graham, and Kenneth Copeland along with a myriad of other secular voices and pastors, all using the lying-for-dollars business plan.

As the rates of change have accelerated, the number of fearful people has dramatically increased. There are two common responses to this fear: white nationalism and Christian nationalism. The first is explicitly racist. The second is characterized by an alliance with a blue-eyed, blond-haired, Aryan Jesus preaching Old Testament derived certainties.

Both groups want to be gatekeepers excluding, perhaps violently, everybody but straight white, males and, perhaps, a few chosen fellow travelers. Perhaps a more fitting metaphor than gatekeeper is the dog fouling the manger without understanding that the horses, cows. and oxen are the reasons the manger is there and full.

A class representative would be Blake Masters, a former senate candidate in Arizona. He talked about people at the border as an "invasion." He argued, "We will lose our country." That statement is a racist dog-whistle about the great replacement theory. One of his last political ads was a video of him wandering around in the desert, trying to look like a good guy with a gun. Essentially, his campaign is trying to generate fear of the other. As Othello found, fear of the other is toxic to Thrivancy.

Blake Masters is a prime example of the mediocrity of the dogs fouling the manger. He is a venture capitalist. He risks other people's money to support things other people are building. He risks little and creates less but feels he is the smartest guy in the room. He would not, indeed probably could not, run for political office without the infusion of millions of dollars from a sugar daddy. A sugar daddy who has spent tens of millions of dollars in an avowed effort to blow up democracy to favor rule by the oligarchs.[11]

Peter Thiel's tens of millions of dollars spent to support Masters is pocket change compared to the single donation of 1.5 billion dollars by Barre Seid to a hard right, Leonard Leo, who engineered the creation of a rogue Supreme Court, and is now leading an effort to "crush liberal dominance" across American life.[12]

> James Baldwin explained why, "Negroes, on the whole, and until lately, have allowed themselves to feel so little hatred. The tendency has really been, insofar as this was possible, to dismiss white people as the slightly mad victims of their own brainwashing."[13 p.102]

Not one of these oligarchs has demonstrated any idea how these immigrants, refugees, and undocumented folks make their lives possible. These are the people who put food on the table, they are the ones building the mansions, or one of the future S&P 500s, 43% of which were founded by immigrants. If they were successful in shutting down the inflow of people, the oligarchs would find it difficult to maintain their lifestyles. The oligarchs build their citadels, sometimes in missile silos and sometimes in New Zealand, fantasizing that, somehow, they are immune to the libertarian Chaos they are trying to create. If they were to succeed, they would quickly come to realize their lives were perched on top of a hierarchy that they worked hard to destroy, that no longer existed, and that no longer functioned for their benefit or protection.

Blake Masters has yet to create the kinds of changes he fantasizes, but other white supremacists have certainly been busy fouling the manger at the national level; witness the rapid creation of a rogue court. After a few years spent eviscerating the right to vote, the Court abrogated fifty years of law, disregarded the writings of Ben Franklin in favor of a British jurist who believed women could be witches, and, in yet another case, totally rewrote the understanding of vigilantism. Six justices all looked through the same narrow tunnel, and thought they were the smartest people in the room. Together, and individually, they are the perfect illustration of the privilege and mediocrity created by white supremacy. It is precisely this level of privileged mediocrity that is driving change dangerous, if not fatal, to the American Idea.

These five drivers of change: the pandemic, climate change, technology, lying-for-dollars, and white supremacy are mutually causal and synergistic. For example, without the in-your-face technology, the lying-for-dollars business plan would not be as profitable and would not have exacerbated the pandemic, nor been able to create the levels of fear required to create the Proud Boys, the Patriot Front, nor the AR-15 idolators.

America is certainly capable of growing our own anti-democratic, right-wing, oligarchs such as Peter Thiel, Barre Seid, and the Koch brothers. But it needs to be said that not all the support or dollars are home grown. There is clear documentation of Russian interference, both financial and propagandistic, in our elections.

It has been suggested, and often documented, that influencers, representatives, senators, cabinet members, and Presidents have been generously supported by an international network with a figurehead of Vladimir Putin. A more recent, and less documented, actor is Mohammed bin Salman of Saudi Arabia. In both cases, the efforts have focused on creating change by

> In the Carlson style, "Just asking the question": How much Russian money has gone directly, or indirectly, to Senator Ron Johnson, Tucker Carlson, or the 'Putin Congressional Beachhead'?"

fraying the social fabric and creating fear of the other; the classic divide and conquer.

The net result is that America, as a nation, is going through paroxysms of social, economic, and spiritual changes with uncertain outcomes. The Country has survived dramatic rates of change in the past: wars, pandemics, assassinations, civil rights, and personal computers; the list goes on. A major difference between then and now is that there were no groups using in-your-face technology to create a dystopian stream of constantly changing sounds and images competing for space in our lives.

Strauss and Howe predicted, "People young and old will puzzle over what it felt like for their parents and grandparents, in a distantly remembered era, to have lived in a society that felt like one national community. They will yearn to recreate this, to put America back together again. But no one will know how." [1p. 252]

The question is, can the American Idea come through this with its identity and function in intact? It is a testament to the country's integrity and Resilience that we have done as well as we have. We have held elections, developed vaccines, responded to climate and earth system catastrophes, led an effective international response to international upheaval, and started paying attention to social justice issues.

However, it is also abundantly clear that large swaths of the country and millions of people have not demonstrated Resilience. They doubled down on responses that were no longer effective except in maintaining the responder's sense of identity. It has always been true that societal responses to novelty and change have been uneven. Every new perspective, added information, or paradigm shift has been met with resistance. History is replete with conflicts between acceptance and rejection of change: heliocentrism, evolution, emancipation, extended suffrage, and recently, Science in general, and vaccinations in particular.

> At the end of WWll, America demonstrated huge if unequal and inequitable resiliency. The net result being massive changes across the country, including rapid growth of the middle class. But that resiliency has faded over time.

One could go on and on. Increasingly ineffective responses have created a multitude of ancillary, unintended consequences that have not increased a sense of control and have not increased thrivancy. A fair question might be why do significant portions of society continue a path of faster, straighter with no deviation in the face of failure? It may be, in fact, they can do no other. It may be, they cannot demonstrate resiliency.

Chapter 3

# What Is Resiliency

Why do we care about whether individuals, institutions, or socio-cultural groups demonstrate Resilience?

Intuitively, it seems worth thinking about and talking about ways to increase individual Resilience. Have any of us come through the global pandemic without having experienced

Doesn't Darwin suggest that if the rate of change exceeds Resilience, extinction follows? That might be true, but very few T-Rexes had AR-15's. People who are not resilient may be armed, frustrated by, and terrified of change. That is not a good combination.

tremendous changes at some level? So much has changed, but somehow, we still need to make life work. We still must eat. We are still searching for some level of security. We still must take care of children, and we still must interact, at some level, in some way, with others.

This is the point where several developing threads start to braid together into a single story. First, the rate of change is unlikely to decrease. Second, the American Middle-class is not thriving. Third, what we are doing is unsustainable and simple solutions will fail.

The first thread is that, absent a history ending Armageddon, the aggregate rates of change will not decrease. COVID-19 is likely to weaken as a change agent, but increased climate change is already baked into the future. It is happening. It is happening as rapidly or more rapidly than predicted and will continue to do so. The socio-cultural ramifications are already being felt and will

About the Supreme Court, if a litigant gave a Justice a gift of $500,000 would that be a bribe?

increase. Technology is accelerating. Who understands or predicts the changes wrought by artificial intelligence?

Once the Supreme Court put *Citizens United* on steroids and permitted the full-on bribery of Texas senators, the future of lying for dollars is huge.[1] Given this court, it is not very far from bribing a senator to bribing a Justice, a cop, a teacher, or in fact anybody you please.

The second thread is that if change is accelerating, it is also making it more difficult for the American Middle-class to achieve or maintain the requisites for resiliency. For the last decade, the percentage of people identified as middle-class has been stable, but they have lost significant financial ground to the upper classes. The middle-class median income rose by 50% from 1970 to 2020 while the upper-class median income rose 69%. In terms of 2020 dollars, the difference is a rise of about $30,000 versus approximately $90,000. The net result is that wealth disparity is mushrooming, and it now takes 53 weeks for the typical male to earn enough income to thrive for 52 weeks. Women must work 66 weeks. In 1985, the numbers were 30 and 45.[2]

A strong middle-class "is a prerequisite for robust entrepreneurship and innovation, a source of trust that greases social interactions and reduces transaction costs, a bastion of civic engagement that produces better governance, and a promoter of education and other long-term investments."[3] A strong American middle-class is a prerequisite for, and a product of, Resilience, and Resilience allows and supports the American Idea.

Thirdly, what was happening is no longer sustainable. The middle class is not thriving; a strong indication that what might have been working is no longer producing the desired results. If something is unsustainable, change is inevitable. We cannot keep on keeping on. We must be resilient.

Resiliency, as a cultural or social goal, is sustainability's child born out of failure. Sustainability was a fringe idea during the sixties and seventies.

> COVID-19 was just one of those things on the far horizon until you lost your job, or a family member, or had to stay home to teach, or were "locked down." A loss of income would certainly focus the mind on rates of change. What you were doing, no longer works.

It didn't really hit mainstream thinking until the eighties when the U.N. finally defined "Sustainable development is development that meets the needs of the present without compromising the ability of future generations to meet their own needs."[4]

At this point, almost half a century later, a broadly based, large scale, sustainable system is not going to happen. It is not possible now, and it has not been possible for a while. Climate change is simply the most visible harbinger of the changes that are beginning to appear in the Earth Systems we all depend on.

The failure of sustainability has been made very clear in the recognition of a continuum of wicked problems that stretch from the Earth systems to social/demographic systems. Thirty, forty, fifty years ago, we had poverty, racism, rankism, environmental degradation, extinction, global heating, food insecurity, and widespread social and economic injustice. Thirty, forty, fifty years ago, very few people seemed to care. These days, there is a dawning realization that the present path to the future is simply untenable; morally, ethically, or physically.

Saying something is a wicked problem is not a value judgment. There is a class of phenomena called wicked problems with the following characteristics:

- They do not have a definitive formulation.

  An example would be a definition of poverty. Is poverty only about finances in all situations? Or is it about command of resources; social, cultural, material? And how do you measure these dimensions across physical or subcultural boundaries?

- Wicked problems do not have a clear, unambiguous resolution.

  Will there ever be a single point where we can say, "We're done; poverty is solved"? The distance between the impoverished and the rich is growing, almost daily in one of the richest countries in the World. Yet we have a state legislator voting against school food programs because he has never met a hungry person in Minnesota. "There are none so blind as those who will not see" and "None so deaf as those who will not hear." This is really about the walls being built between those above and those below.

- All wicked problems, even with the same name, are unique.

  Wicked problems are the products of complex systems where each component has variable degrees of freedom of interaction. The systems producing wicked problems are akin to kaleidoscopes where a relatively few elements can provide many, many outcomes. What this means is poverty in the Southwest is almost certainly not the same as poverty in the Northeast. Rural poverty is never going to be the same as urban poverty; similar but not the same.

- The solutions are not true or false, only better, or worse.

  Given the complicated, complex, and to some extent unknown, nature of the systems producing wicked problems, a single solution will not achieve total success. Is there a single, simple, or complex, end to poverty? Any single solution is a bit like chicken soup. It helps, but it is no cure.

- There is no way to test the solution to a wicked problem.

  It is possible to test a solution to a wicked problem. However, every time a solution is tested, the system that generates the wicked problem is changed. Therefore, the test alters the problem and to some degree, it becomes a new problem. For example, suppose as a requirement for financial assistance, one must be looking for, or have, a job. In parts of rural America, that requirement means you must move into town.

> In rural, southern Oregon, the environment provides housing, heat, water, and food for little cash. Moving down the hill into town for a job meant those benefits cost more cash than available at minimum wage.

Moving into town almost always reduces or removes the ecological services provided by the environment for little or no cash. In town, cash poverty becomes impoverishment. The intervention permanently changes the system and therefore the problem.

- There are always many suggested solutions to a wicked problem.

  A characteristic of wicked problems, the number of elements, the number of people involved, and the lack of strict definitions means many perspectives and solutions. Everybody has an idea. In fact, if everybody agrees to the solution, it is unlikely that we are talking about a wicked problem.

- Wicked problems tend to be connected.

  This is a characteristic that might best be demonstrated simply by asking two questions. Is the problem of poverty somehow a cause and effect of the issues of education? Is there any question that issues of health are related to socio-economic inequities?

Two questions about how to support and grow the Middle-class, and why do we care about the Middle-class represent two facets of a wicked problem.

The question, "Why do we care about the Middle-class?" represents one facet precisely because it is very clear that some parts of America do not care, perhaps because they do not understand nor see the issues. How else can you explain:

- The continuous efforts to gut the safety net of Social Security, Medicare, Obamacare, the child tax credit, etc.

- Changing the rules to protect multi-million dollar checking accounts in failing banks.

- Giving massive tax breaks to the oligarchs and their handmaidens.

- Granting forgiveness for unexamined, unaudited PPP loans.

- Balancing the cost of inflation on the backs of hourly and salaried workers.

- But, somehow, not being able to forgive student loans.

On the other hand, there is a pervasive school of thought that suggests a strong middle-class "is a prerequisite for robust entrepreneurship and innovation, a source of trust that greases social interactions and reduces transaction costs, a bastion of civic engagement that produces better governance, and a promoter of education and other long-term investments."[3] In short, there is no universal recognition that America's Middle class is not thriving, nor is there agreement about whether this matters, or not. Two perspectives with very different opinions make it clear that dealing with the status of the Middle-class is a wicked problem.

The questions about how to support and grow the Middle-class are about both social and economic aspects of the wicked problem. Economically, the zombie, supply-side economic model, with its Laffer Curve, cannot compete with the demand-side model ethically, intellectually, or factually. It absolutely creates inequity and disparity. Both are toxins for the Middle-class.

> Supply-side economics is accurately labelled and described as trickle-down economics. Could you thrive on a trickle of water? Of food? Shelter? Medicine? Money? Survive? Maybe. Thrive? Never.

The Middle-class is supported by demand-side economics. Historically, in the aftermath of WWll, the Middle-class grew rapidly because economic growth was fueled by increased demand characterized:

Economically

- high marginal tax rates on the rich,
- massive infrastructure projects build for the public good,
- low interest rates,
- the G.I bill and, later, the military in general as a nationalized source of education and training.

Socially

- migration to and from urban centers to the suburbs because of subsidized housing,
- reduction in agriculture jobs and increase in unionized manufacturing,
- and perhaps most importantly, some, minimal, acceptance of educational and employment opportunities for women, people of color, and immigrants.

If we want to grow and support American Middle-class thrivancy, we need to stop pumping money, resources, and opportunities upwards and move them laterally. The following sorts of programs would not solve the issues, after all, we are speaking of a wicked problem, but historically, they have proven they would change the problem and make a difference;

- Build and rebuild the degraded American infrastructure including renewable energy systems.

- Independent of other rates, maintain mortgage rates no higher than 4%.

- Increase use of technology to build affordable housing with sustainability and climate change forefront.

- Restore teaching as a respected, well-paid profession.

- Support unionization with access to sick leave, continued job development, and overtime.

- Increase access to day care and pre-school with trained and reasonably paid providers.

- Ensure full-range medical care is accessible to all without bankruptcy nor penury.

If the problems and threats to the American Idea and the Middle-class are wicked, and not clearly defined, we absolutely are going to need Resilience to address them or, indeed, to entertain possible approaches. As we start to think about these issues, it becomes apparent that the required Resilience will have to be at the level of the individual. All Resilience originates with the individual. At all levels, it is the individual who demonstrates Resilience. Institutions, society, and culture can only reflect the resiliency of individuals.

Like COVID-19, and other drivers of change, Resilience is a powerful driver of change. It is not Resilience if one just keeps on keeping on in the face of change. That is the Titanic personified. To simply double down in the face of change is what some political parties, cults, religious organizations, clubs, etc. are doing. Sometime later, but often sooner, that spells extinction.

The development and expression of an individual's Resilience is the product of, and constrained by, a system of components broadly defined as economy, ecology, equity, diversity, and meaning. No two people share precisely the same components in this system because no two people exist in, and experience precisely

> The system structure remains stable even where components are determined by cultural and subcultural identities of racial, gendered, economic, geographic, and spiritual diversity, etc.

the same context. While the specific personal components may vary, and as the individual gets older, probably change, the basic system structure is stable over time.

Surprisingly, the economic components develop earliest. Economics is about the exchange of goods and services. It may involve money, but it often does not. What we see in the early development of Resilience is an economics based on an invisible social capital. Social capital may be invisible but what it buys is not. Social capital buys connections, trust, acceptance, access, opportunity, and contributes to a sense of identity and confidence.[4]

For an infant, the beginning of Resilience is built on the connections with care givers, most often mom, with increasing trust in those connections and the reciprocity that starts to generate confidence, trust, and patience. A toddler without these connections demonstrates less Resilience where the Resilience is manifested in what might be described as a "wait and see" behavior. An infant without the connections settles down to a consistent wail. The infant with the connections, wails and waits to see what happens next. Is this really Resilience? Maybe not, but it is a good first step, and it begins to develop the idea that you are not born resilient. Resilience is learned.

As you mature, three important things happen vis-à-vis social capital. The first change is that the network of connections becomes both denser and more diffuse. If the network can be thought of metaphorically as a set of pipes. The network becomes denser as some pipes, generally short ones, increase in diameter to carry a higher flow and greater variety of interaction. At the same time, some pipes extend farther from the center of the network carrying a lower rate of flow and less variety of interaction. Short, fat pipes connect with the very best friend, and a longer, skinny pipe might connect with the dentist. It is not an either near or far situation. Diameters and lengths are highly variable and changeable over time. Today's fat pipe may shrink to almost nothing. Almost nothing because memories keep the pipe from disappearing; "When we lose someone we love, we must learn not to live without them but to live with the love they left behind."[5]

Second, as the network of connections grows and changes, the economics of social capital come into play. Social capital can only be earned through actions that exchange goods and services. The flow must be reciprocal, and, over time, equal in value but not necessarily in kind. The individual will accrue social capital to the extent that they invest social capital. Without investment, one can occasionally be given the benefits of social capital, essentially by good Samaritans, but that will be rare and not reliable long-term.

Over time, social capital can be banked or saved as reputation and social identity. Your network, both near and far, believes they know who you are. Your social identity and your reputation represent a balance sheet that may be positive, or not, because of investments and ongoing interactions.

Your social identity and reputation can be used to underwrite an intervention or

> The pandemic shrank networks less for women than men. Women maintain networks by talking, men by doing but not talking. "Instead of talking, men 'do things together'. They play sports. They drink. They fish. They play bridge. But they don't talk. The social restrictions brought about by the pandemic have made it very difficult for men to stay connected."[6]

action to bring about change; to underwrite Resilience. Consider two examples. The first example involves two high-school seniors applying to college. They both need recommendations from teachers from their junior or senior year. The first attends a school of 2000 with an average class size of 35 students. The second attends a school of 300 with an average of 20 students per class. The first probably sees a teacher for one class for one year. The second may see the same teacher at least twice, and, if it is a math teacher, maybe three times. With the quality of teachers equal, which student has potentially greater social capital to support a richer, more extensive letter? In this example, more social capital most likely correlates with greater choice and greater choice means potentially greater Resilience.

A correlation between social capital and choice does not always hold. For instance, consider a single, male, middle-aged, assembly line worker with excellent "fix-it" skills, laid off because of COVID-19. He ends up houseless in a tent city. After

> There is a carefully nurtured assumption that there is a positive correlation between social and fiscal capital. If you pose the following situation to urban teenagers: "You are broken down on the side of the road. Two vehicles stop to offer a ride, a shiny new Caddy and a hard-used, older pickup truck. Which do you choose for a ride?" Almost to the person, they say the Caddy. Good money means good people.

he has been in the tent city for some time, he becomes well known for fixing things. When things break in the tent city, you do not call a repair man. They will not come, but he does, and one way or another, he can get things to work again.

His reputation and social identity in the tent city are pure gold, and in the bank. Now COVID-19 is receding, but he cannot get a job. Employers are not looking at the tent city bank. They are looking in the wrong banks, and to them, he is bankrupt and high risk. Without assistance from somebody or some institution, his Resilience is limited, and he cannot intervene to make that change even though he is very rich in social capital.

There is yet another sort of social capital that is very different. In fact, so different, it might be easiest to explain with a thought experiment. Suppose we place a newborn on an island where every need is supplied. Every waste product is removed. There are all kinds of stimuli with trees, and animals, but there is zero interaction with humans. These conditions will produce a "feral child."

There is no way this "forbidden experiment" could be sanctioned. However, it still seems to happen with some frequency in the form of child abuse. Two documented cases involve a boy named Victor of Averyon from the 1780's, and a girl named Genie, a child raised in isolation and silence in Southern California, discovered in 1970.

The people who dealt with and cared for these children after discovery were focused primarily on questions dealing with language acquisition. Could they learn a language at a late date? However, as one reads about the children, and watches videos about Genie, it seems there is an even more fundamental question. Do these children ever develop a full-blown sense of self as in myself?

Robert Fuller argues that the self can only be created through the connection and interaction with others.

> The very name — 'self' — is a misnomer. The term carries strong connotations of autonomy and it's as if it were chosen to mask our interdependence. The self does not stand alone. On the contrary, the autonomous self and individual agency are both illusory. Selves depend on input from other selves to take form and to do anything. Deprived of inputs from others, selves are stillborn. Contrary to the name we call it by, the self is anything but self-sufficient.[7]

It would seem then that social capital can be publicly banked as reputation and identity or privately banked as a fully developed sense of self. An individual's concept of themselves is central to the concept of Resilience. If there were no sense, or a woefully

> There is a distinction between "self" and "role." A role is inherently more culturally or socially defined and limited. The self tends to be more idiosyncratic and generalized across personal contexts.

truncated sense, of the individual's self, what would Resilience be about? The definition of Resilience calls for the maintenance of function and identity in the face of change. Without the sense of self, there is no identity to maintain.

There is an interesting interplay between fiscal capital, i.e., dollars and cents, and social capital. Dollars absolutely make a difference in how much Resilience you might have. With dollars you can buy your way into or out of many situations. The same is true about social capital. The high school senior with less social capital may be able to offset that lack by paying the full cost of schooling. The student richer in social capital, but lacking dollars, may not have as wide a range of choices but may have greater support making those choices work. It is obvious, almost always, the greater your capital balances, the greater potential Resilience you have.

The ecological facet of the resiliency system provides the metaphorical equivalent of the provisioning, regulating, sustaining, and cultural services provided by the biological communities.

Provisioning services would include all the traditional and modern information resources including libraries, the internet, and communications networks about what might be called "news." But even more important would be the availability of diverse village connections including willing mentors and teachers, broadly defined. Provisioning services feed the system with a constant percolation and exchange of information and ideas.

> Ecological services are the under-appreciated basis of our existence. They provide food, water, materials, and medicines. They regulate the physical conditions and processes allowing survival. They sustain the rest of the system and clean up our messes. And they provide cultural sustenance and identity. All without charging a dime.

The regulating services are manifested in cultural, social, and idiosyncratic beliefs, experiences, norms, and, in some situations, rules and regulations. Normally, these components are sufficient to define acceptable Resilience-based interventions or changes an individual might make. Unacceptable change or interventions accrue sanctions. However, sanctions only function to offset benefits. It is the individual's balance between sanctions and benefits that regulates resilient behavior. If sanctions dominate, Resilience is limited. If benefits dominate, Resilience is encouraged.

Sustaining services do not directly affect the individual's potential Resilience. Indirect services provide a basic operating platform for the individual. A sustaining service is about keeping the ecological components functioning and providing stability, a degree of patterning and predictability. Imagine a context where the normal situation is that the immediate future was unknowable. Imagine a context of apparent Chaos: food, no food; water, no water; shelter, no shelter; fear, no fear.

The closer one gets to mere survival in Chaos, the less creative behavior patterns become. In that sort of context, what you have is what you use culturally, socially, physically, technically, and spiritually to maintain or create a response. You do not have the time, nor the resources, to create new approaches or ways of doing something. Resilience is a dream.

Sustaining services are not always the same. For much of America, the term "home" often involves a standard, walled space with a roof. Home does not require walls and a roof. Home is something more than that and something less than that. The way the term is most often used is as a shorthand for a whole range of social, physical, and, perhaps, spiritual services. The cultural myth, not always true but always dreamt of, is when the individual is home, the self is known and appreciated, social capital is abundant, the ecological services are sufficient and the potential for Resilience is supported.

> Home can be huge, or it can be tiny. You can be home in the middle of a wilderness, an NFL stadium, a political rally, a church, or temple, or on the sofa in the family room before dinner.

This kind of home may be a single spot or a residence. Home can also be much larger, a neighborhood, town, city, region. or even a country. Large or small, the kind of familial or social home where Resilience would thrive is likely to have the following dimensions:

Appreciation

- There are accessible spaces in the community that offer natural and crafted beauty.
- Community celebrations feature public appreciation for community success stories.

Generosity

- People know others in the community they can offer help to and request help from.
- People share and volunteer their talents and stories with others in the community.

Interest

- There are always new things and people to discover in the community.

- There are classes, workshops, and learning events available in the community.

> This is easy to describe for a community, but the dimensions could be scaled, and applied, up or down, changing as needed, from nation to apartment.

Lightness

- There is evidence of spontaneous interactions and gatherings in the community.

- It is common to see smiles, hear live music and see children playing in the community.

Easy

- People have easy access to good schools, health care, jobs, and fresh food and water in the community.

- It is easy for visitors and residents to find what they look for in the community.[8]

The final sort of ecological services are the cultural services supporting the development of identity and meaning. The local ecology may provide opportunities and resources for inspirational, educational, recreational, spiritual, and aesthetical identities and meanings. Having the phrase, "knee high by the 4th of July," roll off your tongue may identify your age, and background. If somebody speaks knowledgeably about "Sierra Cement," they are telling you something about their history and what they do for fun.

> A way to think about cultural services is to think about their absence. Tourists are in a cultural space where they have little or no experience. They are rootless, without identity, and few or no connections. Absent a good Samaritan, their Resilience is essentially nil. They come, they go, they are a cipher, the opposite of a citizen.

Do the citizens of any other city identify with the "J-Pod"? Probably not, but a common hallmark of Seattle metro residents is a focus on the health and welfare of the J-Pod Orcas. It is part of a broad cultural identity. The environment, large and small, clearly shapes and forms our cultural identities.

These four ecological services, provisioning, moderating, sustaining, and cultural, provide the cocoon that allows Resilience to develop. Absent one or more of these services, Resilience will be much more difficult, if not impossible, to fully develop

Equity is an important element in the Resilience system. Here, equity has the very specific meaning that no resilient action or response will have externalized costs borne by those, human or other, that do not benefit from the action. If there are externalized costs, i.e., subsidies, Resilience will fail, financially, socially, or ecologically bankrupted.

The prime examples of inequitable choices are the tragedies of the commons. If I decide to live an hour out of the city and commute five days a week in a private car, the direct externalized costs of that decision involve at least the various air and water pollutions. The indirect subsidies involve ecological damage of getting oil out of the ground, refining, and transporting it to me. At an even greater distance, there is an inequity involving all the ramifications of the acidified ocean.

> Is it possible to achieve equity? Perhaps, at a small scale, it might be possible. Extreme examples of off-grid homesteading might get close to equity. But even that is open to debate. Therefore, in the case of equity, it must be about minimizing inequities. To modify a cliché, "Do not let perfect be the enemy of much, much better."

A reasonable response to this example might be, really? Is my commute causing all this inequity? No, my single car probably does not contribute a significant bit to the issue. But the automobile system, of oil, mining, concrete, carbon dioxide, and all the rest of it is being subsidized by peoples' health, mass-extinctions, and a general diminishment of all four ecological services. To the extent that I decide on that commute, I contribute in a tiny but real way to the system's coming bankruptcy and death. An act of resiliency must either achieve or work towards equity to be sustainable and successful.

Diversity, or having multiple types of each class of components in the system, will play a significant role in setting the upper limits of an individual's Resilience. Diversity would include, but not be limited to, multiple sources of social capital, a broad array of information sources including people, and a variety of social, intellectual, and physical skill sets.

A single source of social capital essentially means you are an indentured servant. If we have only one source, we cannot take the risk of alienation, aggravation, or isolation. We cannot just up and leave. Under these circumstances, individual Resilience is so limited as to be close to nonexistent without the intervention of a good Samaritan.

A single information source would be a frightening situation. No single source, human or otherwise, can deliver the kind of richness, complexity, or completeness that multiple sources with multiple perspectives can provide for even simple situations. Multiple discrete sources provide more information, and more potential paths of Resilience. A real and present danger to cultural and personal Resilience at this moment is the control of more and more national and local media concentrated in the hands of six or seven oligarchs.

> Different sources put it different ways, but the consensus is that 6 CEO's control about 90% of American Media. Clear Channel, or iHeartMedia, claims to reach 90% of all Americans each month.[9]

The efficacy of having multiple social, intellectual, and physical skill sets in determining potential levels of Resilience is straight forward. Social skill sets might include code switching or having some facility in two or more languages. The way you use language builds bridges or walls, either of which modify levels of Resilience.

Diversity of intellectual skills might include being able to understand, analyze, and evaluate information from a variety of sources, styles, vocabularies, and technical contents. It might include being able to put together effective search strings for the internet. Perhaps the preeminent skill would be to be able to communicate new, complex ideas and concepts effectively.

In terms of physical skills, the old cliché, "If the only tool you have is a hammer, pretty soon everything looks like a nail," is a succinct summary. The different skill sets combine and multiply each other. If you know geometry, have the requisite manual skills, and can communicate your ideas and needs to others, you can lash together an effective shelter in a short period of time. Geometry will help keep it from collapsing. The manual skills will allow you not to do damage to yourself and others, nor waste material, and the social skills will allow communication and cooperation.

In all three cases, increasing diversity of social capital inputs, information sources, and skills, has reduced the effect any single component has on the individual's Resilience. Increased diversity means development of Resilience is no longer concentrated or located at a single spot in the network but becomes diffused across multiple components and connections.

As sources of capital come and go, as information flows or not, as skills are gained and lost, the locus of control moves across the network sometimes here, sometimes there, sometimes linked to a specific component and sometimes diffused across multiple connections. The overall result of component diversity in the system is a net increase in choice by the individual. Thereby increasing both resiliency and thrivancy.

Meaning is a powerful source of control on Resilience. If Resilience is the ability to maintain identity and function in the face of change, meaning defines the range of possibilities. At this moment in time, the existence of COVID-19 vaccines triggers a broad range of different meanings for people. For some, vaccines mean safety. Some see coercion, and some see flat-out evil, or danger. The meaning assigned to the vaccines makes vaccination certain, or possible, or not.

The assignment of meaning happens in three steps. The first step is to identify something as information. Information is a difference that makes a difference.[10] Things change constantly, but if it makes no difference, it is not information.

The second step is to assign meaning to that difference using a socially shared, or personal, code. A social code "is a set of shared understandings among users about the relationship between a symbol and the thing symbolized. A cultural group or community can be thought of as a group of people who share a common system of codes."[11]

> An individual's codes are part of self-definition. A changed code can change that definition as a Christian, or Muslim, or male, or female. There is a link between the development, and acceptance of codes, and the development and acceptance of the Self.

A code may be simple, for instance, the Morse Code, or complex, such as any of the major religions. The Morse Code illustrates an important part of paradigms. They are all limited. You can transcribe incoming code rapidly and accurately and not have a clue if you do not understand the language. Part of any education, training or development is learning where paradigm boundaries lie, and where they can be extended.

Meaning does not exist in a vacuum. Meaning always occurs in a context. As an example, consider the old joke, what is the meaning of a verbal statement, "There is a man eating fish"? Is it a shark or a guy enjoying dinner? For a less hackneyed example, consider the following set of statements:

- The Universe exists.
- The door slamming in the middle of the night is real.
- But the slamming door may be a very different thing for me than you, perhaps hopeful vs. hopeless.

- The difference is not in the door. It is in the connections made to other realities.

- Therefore, meaning resides in connections, not things.

- The creation and assignment of meaning is most often a shared, social process of negotiation and agreement about connections.

- If the process is totally idiosyncratic, it may be insanity or genius.

The outcome of the process of negotiation would be a shared code including a set of rules, definitions, assumptions, concepts, values, practices, and connections that allow one to assign meaning, or not, to the constant flow of inputs, stimuli, and experiences of their reality. This is the definition of a paradigm. A shared paradigm is a shared understanding of a pattern.

The pattern may be as limited as the process for making wonderful French bread. It could be a bit broader as in the general process, standards, and approaches we use to interact with our co-workers. Any of the World's religions would be an example of a broadly shared, extensive, and complex paradigm.

Because meanings are embedded in, and arise from contexts and patterns, paradigms are crucial to the development of Resilience. The degree of Resilience based on one paradigm is inherently more limited than a Resilience that can draw from multiple paradigms. The more paradigms one has at their disposal, the more potential sources of choice, and therefore more Resilience one has.

Everybody has and uses multiple shared paradigms. As we go through the day, we constantly shift paradigms as we deal with different tasks, individuals, groups, and contexts. A pervasive, broadly shared, pattern that includes or subsumes multiple less extensive patterns may be called by several different names, including culture or worldview.

An example of a common, pervasive, American, white, male, cultural, paradigm might be summarized as:

- Humans are at the pinnacle, not Nature.

- There is a natural hierarchy of the fit and unfit; both in humans and Nature.

- The free-willed, self-controlled, independent individual is responsible and sacrosanct.

- Human fitness and value can be quantified economically through competition.

- There is always room at the top for one more fit individual, assuming certain social qualifications.
- Newtonian mechanics pretty much rules the visible Universe.
- A linear, *post hoc, propter hoc,* reductionist analysis provides effective problem solving.
- A strictly utilitarian, low value, commodification of the less-fit and non-human makes sense.

This is a hierarchical view of the World. There are a few people at the top of the pyramid followed by widening classes of others, including less-fit people, cultures, races, animals, and plants. At the base is the physical planet. This cultural paradigm is certainly not reflective of the breadth of America. However, this is not a paradigmatic equivalent of a straw man. Each of these statements is supported by any search of anecdotes, headlines, or internet sites.

A large, perhaps dominant, percentage of white, male, Americans will find themselves in agreement with all, or most, of these statements. Agreed, this is painted with a broad brush. Variations in contents, emphasis, valuation, and confidence are going to be found, but the core concepts will be similar across a broad swath of the American white male population.

A paradigm functions as a filter. We are constantly immersed in or, more properly, swamped by a constant stream of stimuli. Imagine if you had to spend your time paying attention to the details of the deluge. Imagine if you really had to analyze and think about how everything fits together and what it meant. A paradigm takes care of that. A paradigm automatically assigns a connection and meaning to the stimuli as they arrive. Without a functioning paradigm, you would have no time, no energy, and no capacity to do anything else. We become habituated to much of that stream and ignore almost all the rest. Only some tiny fraction of that stream can be registered consciously.

For instance, if you drive from work to home 150 to 200 times a year, you probably say, "I know the route to get home." You have a paradigm that allows you to get home. The first time you drove the route, even as an experienced driver, you probably paid attention to a broad range of inputs from a wide radius. You saw the stop lights, and the crosswalks as new inputs. You may have paid a great deal of attention to how others were negotiating the same terrain. You may have admired the buildings and registered the shops and many other details as you went.

After you have driven the same route a hundred or two hundred times, you pretty much drive it on the radar. You make assumptions about how other cars are going to behave. You can assume that the yellow lasts the usual amount of time before turning red. You make thousands of assumptions that today is just like the day before and the day before that. You only pay attention to unexpected blips or events, and the road leads you home.

> The road leads you home. If you closed your eyes at any turn, would you know when to spin the wheel to make the next turn? Would you really know how far to turn the wheel to navigate the corner? Your experience allows you to translate what the road communicates. Even though the inputs vary day-to-day, hour-to-hour, the response is almost automatic.

The filtering and blocking of stimuli under these circumstances is huge. If that massive filtration were not happening, could you get home? Can you remember when you were behind the wheel, alone, for the first time? If it was in traffic, do you remember how exhausting that experience was? The situation is parallel with all paradigms. Once learned, translations can be automatic, saving time and energy.

It is not an insult to say we spend most of our day on radar. Imagine the sort of psychic exhaustion that would occur if all the potential impacts of all the potential stimuli poured into your brain. Survival depends on filtering out virtually all those stimuli.

What kinds of stimuli do you get through these filters? For the most part, what gets through are bits of information, differences that make a difference.[12]

How do we identify the stimuli that represent a difference that

> If you have a bag of 200 M&M-like candies, and I told you I added one, it will not make a difference. Knowing there are about two hundred is close enough, If I tell you I put a camouflaged pebble in the bag, that will get through the filter. It makes a difference. That is information.

makes a difference? How do we deal with an overwhelming phantasmagoria? We start to construct a filter, even while we are in the womb,[13] that allows a tiny fraction of potential stimuli to get through.

When we are young, we are shown the filters. We are shown, this is important, that is not. This is valuable, that is not. This is true, that is not. This is dangerous, that is not. This is how you do this. These are the rules about that.

Some of this we are told. Much more, we learn by imitation. We absorb the culture, worldview, or paradigm we are immersed in just by living it. The greater part is rarely expressed in words and therefore rarely made explicit or examined.

Because most often, the contents are not explicit, nor examined, it is

> During the Vietnam war, some draftees claimed pacifism. Almost always denied when a guy on the draft board would ask, "If somebody were killing your mother, would you fight to kill?" Of course, the answer is yes. Family is almost always the top American value and, in some contexts, overrides all others, even devout pacifism.

entirely possible to have conflicting or contradictory elements. It is entirely possible to hold simultaneously incompatible beliefs because broadly applicable cultural paradigms are not monolithic. They will contain context-specific, often conflicting minor paradigms.

One of the crucial lessons we learn, and relearn, is when to use, or not use, a particular paradigm. As a trivial example, using the standard, reductionist "Science" paradigm to analyze the structure and process of any church service is not likely to work very well. On the other hand, using any one of the spiritual or religious paradigms to analyze an internal combustion engine is going to be equally fruitless.

Many pages back, personal Resilience was defined as maintaining one's self-identity and function in the face of change. Resilience happens when we learn these lessons about the efficacy of different responses based on alternative paradigms, large and small, through exploration and feedback. We try out different interventions in response to a change and see what happens. This is feedback and no system can persist without it.

For the individual, the general term "feedback" might include pain or discomfort but more frequently addresses some versions of the following sorts of questions:

- Did I carry out the action properly and well?
- Is the outcome what I expected? If not, why not?
- Is the outcome what I needed or wanted? If not, what has changed?
- What was my social capital cost or gain in this action?

The answers to these questions are a major source of reinforcement, or not, of the paradigm used to shape the response. If the answers to the questions are not the desired answers, the individual may decide to try the same thing again only more so, or there may be a change in tactics based on choosing a different paradigm. This process shapes the contents of the individual's Resilience.

This is the Resilience system that produces and limits the existence of an individual's Resilience. It is a complex system because very few, if any, connections between the components are of the "on / off" type. If you run mental experiments about the connections between any two, three, or four of the system components, it becomes clear the relationships are nonlinear.

Most of the connections might be described by a combination of equations akin to "If X, then Y, Else Z or 0." Even if we could know everything about the contents of an individual's Resilience system, it would be impossible to make anything more than general statements about possible outcomes. Metaphorically, this system is akin to a kaleidoscope. A bit of a twist and a whole new pattern emerges. This is a system operating, just as it should, on the edge of Chaos.

Chaos is not random. It is unpredictable in the details, but it is possible to move the system in the direction of greater Resilience. The multiple impacts of poverty on the early development of the system in the first years of life has been documented.[14] However, the same report strongly indicates that the early effects can be offset, and the system can be moved in the direction of increased levels of Resilience.

> It is not just children trapped by a single paradigm. The World is full of stories of adults, trapped in a single paradigm, being reintroduced to other paradigms. See Tom Hanks in *A Man Called Otto.*

If the goal is to increase the degree of American cultural Resilience, a place to start would be the creation of a new educational paradigm incorporating the Resilience system. Because schools and schooling are so central in so many communities, American cultural Resilience would rapidly increase and spread.

# Chapter 4

# Paradigm Development and Function

COVID-19 has changed the World. The disruptions, the interruptions, the corruptions, the isolations, the deaths, the grief, the mourning, the uncertainty, and the decay of the community have just created a mess. Some people, institutions, and segments of society seem to have been relatively untouched. Some segments of society have managed to adapt, sometimes after hard work and some courage. A significant segment of our society has not adapted. In the face of significant, broad change, they keep on keeping on, at enormous, inequitable, personal, social, and cultural costs.

To some degree, this situation can be explained by a lack of information, too much misinformation, and a steady flow of disinformation. Facebook, Fox News, and Newsmax have been very effective launching sites for a constant, fire-hose stream of disinformation and misinformation; in short, lying. What seems counter-intuitive is that all this misinformation leads to the increased death and destruction of the direct audience rather than the bystanders or onlookers.

> This behavior is based on part of the American cultural paradigm: Human fitness and value can be quantified economically through competition. There is no morality or ethics involved in spreading misinformation or disinformation to those lower in the hierarchy.

As the Covid variants surged, it became a pandemic of the direct audience, the unvaccinated, often rural, frequently evangelical, and increasingly young. The explanation for this counter intuitive behavior on the part of the liars is the immediate influx of dollars. Lying pays well. Long-term, maybe not so much, but short term, lying provides a bonanza.

The dominant, white, male, cultural, paradigm as described has been under development for a long time as the result of a process of privatization of the commons, development of property law applied to chattel slavery, and maintenance of penury through social control[11]. Officially, chattel slavery has ended, to be replaced by Jim Crow and overt racism. The privatization, development of property law, and social control continue apace.

Much of it was codified starting in the mid-1600's with the definition of who was or was not a slave. For about 300 years, the white proto-oligarchs of America protected their positions socially, financially, and legally, passing laws that defined who was human and who was not, who was property and who was not, who counted and who did not. This process has been documented, in detail, by Lisa Sharon Harper in *Fortune*[9], and by Keri Leigh Merritt in *Masterless Men.*[10] The process was slowed by the civil war but certainly not stopped. An abundance of lynchings demonstrated that.

More recently, the paradigm has been defended in two major wars. The defense by "The Greatest Generation" was heroic, sacrificial, and extraordinary. It was all of that, but they never quite figured out what they were fighting for. They returned home and operationalized the American paradigm in ways that legalized racism, misogyny, rankism, and white privilege. Their children, the Boomers, a few of whom became hippies, made some attempt at breaking down the racism and sexism, but never abdicated the throne of white, male privilege.

Today, the process continues. The Boomers, some of their children, and a scattering of their grandchildren are legislating hundreds of new laws to disenfranchise the lower incomes, those with darker complexions, and those who do not quite fit. Lynching people recently became a federal hate crime, but it is an okay thing to string up the fundamental rights of those who might threaten the porcine throne of white male privilege. Republican dominated legislatures have legislated and gerrymandered the heart out the voting franchise with able assistance from the politicians in robes.

The net result of the legalizing and socializing of the paradigm was a truncating of the rest of the Resilience system. The most segregated and isolated group in America are white males. They can live for days, perhaps weeks, without exposure to any alternative paradigms. Their lives have become impoverished in so many ways. The sources of social capital become limited. Concepts of equity, in terms of externalized costs, are truncated. Valuation of intellectual and physical skills becomes narrowed. Dollars became the primary arbiter of value. Sources of meaning, including spirituality, became narrowed, politicized, and weaponized.

Those who function within this dominant white male paradigm do not recognize how impoverished they are. It is as though people such as Justice Alito are looking at the World with a narrow tunnel vision that might be called "The Alito Straw." While some knowledge bases are doubling, the Alito knowledge base shrinks back to the 1300's. Wicked problems simply do not exist in this view. The result is an almost comical intellectual, spiritual, and psychologically truncated concept of reality. Justice Alito and the captain of the Titanic have so very much in common.

The process continues. "Tennessee is one of 11 states this year that have drastically curtailed the ways that districts can fight systemic and individual acts of racism, homophobia, and sexism in the classroom and how teachers can talk to students about the ways America's government has historically discriminated against minorities."[1] If a teacher were to cross the line to teach about systemic racism, sexism, and homophobia, the district could be fined between one and five million dollars. The Titanic kept on keeping on and a great many died, slow, lonely deaths.

The pace quickens. The rogue Supreme Court has taken the first giant step to deny the Federal Government the ability to promulgate regulations such as the clean air, or water act, or, in fact, any regulations. The politicians on the Supreme Court have been busy taking away voting rights and is now considering the idea that state election decisions by legislatures cannot be challenged in the courts.[2] So, individual states are busy disenfranchising women, people of color, and urban folks. After all, if Justice Alito can use the "Alito Straw," so can the white boys in the state legislatures.

Unfortunately, the Supreme Court's decisions are no longer limited to the U.S.A. Their decisions on the ability of the Federal Government to regulate issues such as climate change and public health will have reverberating global impacts. As the impacts spread, people will die, people will be killed, and societies will unravel globally and locally. Millions of unnecessary deaths will be the net result of the Justices'

> The SCOTUS is losing public respect. As it should. "The six" are perjurers, two are sexual predators, at least three have been bought on the open market, and one is a fence post turtle. They are perfect examples of the mediocrities produced by the dominant white male cultural paradigm.

lack of intellectual breadth and depth in support of Resilience.

This is no longer Captain of the Titanic. The Court has become the cultural equivalent of the Captain of Hindenburg. With their abandonment of *stare decisis,* i.e. to stand by things decided, to achieve their ends, they have the capacity to just burn the American Idea, and the rest of the World, to the ground.

The point has been made multiple times but needs repetition here. All this dismemberment, decay, and destruction of the American Idea is happening because the dominant white, male, cultural, paradigm has devolved into an ideology. It answers all the questions, all the time, and brooks no interference.

The ideology has driven other paradigms into the cultural hinterlands. We have lost the Resilience based on alternative paradigms to address the wicked problems of the day. Some of those wicked problems range from natural outcomes of history, and some of those problems are generated, on purpose, by the scavenger oligarchs.

As the Boomers fade, they deserve the disapprobation they get from the rising generations. The question becomes, how do we support Gen Z and those who follow, in their efforts not to have an endless replay of what we have now? We will have more pandemics. The oligarchs, both local and global, will continue to foment the breaking of society into warring camps. As a culture, we must respond to those who wish to exacerbate issues of inequity and unequal opportunity. To put it forcibly, how do we make it possible for Gen Z and their allies to blow up the porcine throne of white, male, privilege?

The short answer is we do it by spending the time, effort, and resources applying what we know to rebuild the institutions designed to create individual Resilience. The even shorter answer is we invest what we know into educating the young. The shortest answer is we use the village to teach.

I will be using "teacher" as shorthand for those in front of the formal or informal classroom, in front of an expeditionary program, and in front of their children or grandchildren. The shorthand includes policy makers, or others mentoring, coaching, supporting or in any other fashion involved with enhancing or helping others: parents, pastors, sergeants, captains, mayors, council members, service club members.

Virtually every one of us at some time or other is a teacher. Is there really anybody who is not at least a part time teacher? The following discussion focuses on formal schooling, but most of what is said applies to the broadest definition of "teacher."

Before we get to what must be done to support and enhance the American Idea, and the development of Resilience, it is important to understand how, and why, teachers, and schooling have failed to do so in the past. That we have failed is manifest in the Chaos, disruption, and just extraordinary behavior of a significant portion of the population in response to the pandemic.

Parents rebelled against mask mandates in elementary schools where vaccines could not be given because of student age. Segments of the adult population accepted and fervently believed ludicrous ideas; vaccines make you magnetic, vaccines contain future controlling micro-chips, and the big one, after achieving 700,000 pandemic deaths, that the vaccine was more dangerous than the disease, and that the virus could be routed by taking horse de-wormer.

The pandemic was the headline-generator, but it was not the only source of stress. We had the whole cast of Fox News, starring Tucker Carlson, perfecting the lying for dollars business model. They fed their greed and America got misled.

> During the pandemic, the collective net worth of the oligarchs grew by $931 billion while middle-class unemployment broke records.[3]

It takes a village to raise a child. Isn't that the old cliché? And isn't it true that the village is rapidly diminishing? Every day, schools and teachers are being formally, and informally, tasked with picking up the responsibilities that in the past were dealt with by at-home parents, extended multigenerational families, neighborhoods, local churches, service organizations, and the networks all those elements imply. As the village fades, teachers become more and more central to the present and the future of the student.

To address the moral, ethical, and physical issues of poverty, racism, rankism, environmental degradation, extinction, global heating, food insecurity, and widespread social and economic injustice, we must change our approach to schooling and education. With limited cultural Resilience, the American Idea is unlikely to survive in the face of cultural and social Chaos. The success of schools and schooling in supporting Resilience can be increased by re-integrating the village into the process of teaching.

The immediate question then becomes why the village left the educational system. There are likely as many answers as you wish to discover but two of the more important come down to suburbanization and Sputnik.

For over 60 years, since the Russians launched Sputnik, we have been afraid of falling behind Russia and the rest of the World in terms of military prowess, technology, gold medals, and education. We have constantly been driven to do more.

With the vision of Sputnik looming overhead, we have been through wave after wave of school reform to achieve more and more as the village fades. Initially, the white males in charge decided that teachers, mostly female, were unqualified and untrained, especially in the Sciences. So, education and schooling became text-centric. Textbooks, especially science books, went from monochromatic, text-based, rather dull efforts to technicolor, visually replete, multi-faceted, all-incorporating volumes that assumed the teacher was primarily a traffic director.

Until publishing and technology caught up, textbooks became expensive to develop and buy. That meant fewer texts were available. Biology in upstate New York became the same as Biology in the State of Texas, as did the rest of the curriculum, including History. Since the turn of the century, the influence and limits of textbooks have receded. These days, with ubiquitous computers and the internet in schools, libraries, and homes, teachers and many students have all kinds of alternative curricula, information sources, and assistance readily available. If teachers, parents and/ or students have the time and resources, Texas can once again be different from New York, but it takes dedication and a great deal of work.

In spite of the best efforts of those sorts of individuals, the death-knell for localized schooling came with the rise of the second wave of reform, test-centric schooling. We teach to the test. Everybody says we do not, but we do, often implicitly and sometimes explicitly as in the A.P and IB programs. Much of this reform is a direct outgrowth of the American cultural paradigm that you can rank an individual's fitness using a number, and a higher number, automatically indicates a more fit person.

Measuring fitness by a test score has become supercharged with the spread of Advanced Placement classes. The classes are pressurized by the existence of a single nationwide exam administered, graded, and reported by strangers. While accomplished, master, teachers might put a personal spin on them, the contents of History or Science courses once again became the same in New York and Texas.

The text-centric and the test-centric reforms were both conceptually simple responses to Sputnik. They certainly changed teaching. There were unintended consequences including, but not limited to, homogenized schools and education, the impoverishment of Art and Music, and a failure to put higher numbers on test scores.

Education and schooling turn out to be wicked problems connected to changes in the rest of the social, economic, and ecological fabric. When considering the role of schools in the creation of Resilience, an important connection is to the growth of the suburbs.

> In the late 1940s and 50s, the GI Bill and Levittown clones generated a rapid growth of suburbs with influx from both sides; urban and rural. Dad off to work, mom at home, modest house, picket fence, "Leave it to Beaver" became a vision of the American Dream. A vision that remains while the reality has changed.

Back in the day, before the suburbanization of the late 40s, early 50s, students could leave school daily and participate in a real, economically significant, way in the community and often in the family.

As the suburbs expanded and work moved farther from home, school became more central to student lives and students became more separated from the broader cultural stage. The village started to fade. To some extent, in a suburban school, after-school sports, bands, etc. replaced working with dad or mom in the shop, or Uncle Bill on the truck farm, or any other close-in village occupations. The fading village and increased age-grade isolation from the broader cultural context impacted the contents of the Resilience system on at least two dimensions, economics and ecological services.

Social capital is necessary to underwrite an individual's Resilience. Social capital can only accrue through action and reciprocity. Schools are less complicated, less complex, and inherently less diverse theaters for action than the surrounding community. No school, no classroom, no mentoring or coaching situation could tolerate the breadth of action, interaction, or inaction found in even the least complex community.

The net result of spending more time on campus is a reduction in the diversity of social capital resources. The on-campus student interacts with a narrower range of adult roles, perspectives, and actions. Teachers in any given school probably mostly share similar worldviews, values, and backgrounds. The racial make-up of the faculty is likely to be less diverse than the student body. Because of fewer opportunities off campus, the school personnel become more important but more limited, sources of social capital.

A second source of social capital, the peer group, is second only to parents in the underwriting of the development of the self. Again, the student body is inherently less diverse in age, experience, and perspectives than the group the student would meet as an active member of a broader community. And can we just stipulate students in groups are not always the best judges of the good, the bad, and the ugly? The *Lord of the Flies* may be extreme, but not entirely wrong. It is a blessing that graduation is a rite of passage where the peer-generated visions of self can be abandoned. In any case, that vision of school-self is important in school, and often invisible outside of it.

Even the best, most progressive, liberated, and humane schools inherently limit options to effectively earn social capital. As the village fades and schools become more central to students' lives, the opportunities to earn social capital become more constrained, less diverse, more socio-economically homogenous, and more limiting.

The Ecological services available to the student will be modified by school attendance. The sustaining services, those not actually about teaching but supporting the effort, may be more effective at school than in the fading village. Close to fifteen percent of all American children under eighteen live in poverty. In the major cities, the child poverty rate from North to South, East to West, varies but is often above forty percent.

Poverty is food insecurity. Poverty and near-poverty parents often work one or two jobs that are often physically exhausting, dangerous, and demoralizing. Fixing three meals a day in many cases, is an unrealized, and unaffordable, dream. A quickie burger, fries, and a shake are going to

> For McDonald's, raising prices 20% in two years has led to a downturn in visits from lower-income consumers earning about $45,000 a year or less, CEO Chris J. Kempczinski told investors during the chain's third-quarter earnings call on 11/13/23.

cost less than trying to put together the same number of nutritious calories at the grocery chain.

The number of schools that make good food available, often with inadequate facilities, limited budgets, and limited personnel, twice, and sometimes three times a day to kids is staggering, and they carried on through the pandemic.

Despite recurrent efforts to limit school lunches, and to make ketchup a vegetable, they are an important support in every community. Food, along with clean hot and cold water, heating and cooling, perhaps a modicum of medical supervision, and a relatively safe space is one of those things that formal schooling does well. As much as anything else the school does, these supports are

> Schools provide these services twelve months a year in many creative and wonderful ways. One of the early "feel good" stories of the pandemic was about how schools continued to feed kids even when the schools were shut. An even better story is the number of states starting to feed every student every day.

a net gain in the potential Resilience of students.

The ecological regulating services for an on-campus student are most likely to be more constraining than those in the broader village. Very few village denizens run their days in 45- or 50-minute blocks regulated by bells. No matter where the students go on a K-12 campus, they are very likely to be seen, watched, and observed by one or more rule-keepers, i.e., adults. There is generally a rule of some sort that can be applied for every event, every moment, on campus.

The net result is that exploration, experimentation, and adventure are channeled in ways acceptable to both adults and students at the school. The channels change over time, and no two schools have precisely the same channels, but they will always be more limited than the village channels. Off campus, a student can disappear for a while, and act in ways for which there are no rules or regulations.

The provisioning services and cultural services rendered by the school are so tightly connected it is sometimes difficult to see where one starts or the other ends. In terms of provisioning, schools provide teachers, mentors, perhaps nurses, counselors, and coaches of various sorts. Most often schools provide hardware, software, connectivity, and access to digital or print resources, external sources of expertise, entertainment, and skills. And, schools provide a plan, a road map of how to get through the day, the week, the year, and, with luck, life.

These provisioning services are what one sees when walking through the campus: the teachers, the computer and science labs, the library, fields, theaters, class spaces, etc. What is harder to see are the cultural services being rendered by the school. Cultural services are intangible and involve aesthetics, including a sense of identity, pride in belonging, of "we-ness" and "them-ness," and a sense of continuity between past and future.

These provisioning and cultural services are important parts of the inputs that create a student's sense of self. The school nurtured self is not particularly stable. It can be, often is, shuffled off as the student walks out the door, but it does serve as a launching pad for further development. Important as it may be, this input and development cannot be as varied as the inputs from the village. As the suburban school became more isolated, the cultural inputs tend to become more homogenous and limited.

These three ecological services, support, regulation, and provisioning, are important to the development of student Resilience. If any one of those is missing or limited, then the system becomes truncated and limited; less opportunity to earn social capital, less diversity in technical and social skills, and less stability. However, none of these is as pervasive and crucial to the development of Resilience as the cultural services provided by the school.

Schools may appear similar or the same, the computers might be the same, the library might have mostly the same books, and the teachers might look the same. But a school in the Bronx, a school in Houston, a school in coastal Maine, and a school in coastal Oregon will have different cultural services that color and transform the road maps for students. Schools with huge budgets and schools with tiny budgets all stretch their budgets to create a unique, almost trademark, cultural identity.

There are two closely related but slightly different ways in which cultural services can be debilitating and claustrophobic.

The first is what might be called the marshmallow model. No matter where you look inside a marshmallow, from front to back, it is featureless, and uniform. It may be that it is a very benign marshmallow, but it will not generate Resilience. There will be minimal diversity anywhere in challenges, or perspectives, or in alternative paradigms. Or even in any differences that make a difference. In a marshmallow school, every perspective looks out on the same featureless view.

Are there schools exactly like that? Probably not, but there are certainly schools that are trending towards that end of the continuum. Some of the schools with national reputations have what might be called cookie-cutter students in abilities, intelligences, and learning styles taught by a faculty with uniform perspectives prepared by liberal arts colleges with abilities, intelligences, and learning styles mirroring the students. Such schools may be academic powerhouses, but they are not necessarily bastions of Resilience.

The second cultural model would include schools broadly defined as religious or cultish. In this case, there may be a diversity of students, teachers, and contexts, but there is only one perspective, one paradigm, one leader, and one source of Truth. In short, all the answers, all the time, are the same.

> An interesting conundrum is the thought that the difference between a good school and an excellent school is not likely to be what is taught or how it is taught. The difference between a good school and a truly excellent school is more likely found in what is not taught.

Examples would include radical religions of all types, creeds such as white supremacy, or allegiance to some figurehead, secular savior, politician, or hallowed tradition. What makes this situation claustrophobic is that questions are heresies. Lacking questions means that answers and responses tend over time to spiral ever inward and become ever more rigid and inviolate.

While this sounds extreme, there are schools trending in that direction: the racial or social segregation academies, the high school football factories, the wannabe Saint Grottlesex schools, or the local, test-centric high school. Everybody in the village loves to see those test scores go up based on questions that everybody accepts as correct, true, and fit the social paradigm.

> These days, there are vociferous efforts to create "anti-woke" schools. In these schools, race, LGBTQIA+, History, books, white-discomfort, and questions will not exist. These will be the ultimate marshmallow schools, and Resilience will fade.

Can you imagine a national AP History test question on My Lai? Or a biology test question about the impact of agricultural antibiotics? Or an English essay question to develop a position on the most important dimension of citizenship?

You probably cannot because that will not happen for a very long time, if ever. To the extent a school becomes test-centric, local perspectives, place-based programs, Art, Music, and individualism tend to fall away. Everybody learns the same material in the same way. The danger is that the school tends to become an institution based on the creed and hallowed traditions of the dominant white, male cultural paradigm.

The present-day brouhaha over Critical Race Theory (CRT) precisely proves the point. The critiques of CRT are rarely even loosely tied to the definition as "a way of looking at law's role platforming, facilitating, producing, and even insulating racial inequality in our country."[4] If that sounds like a subject that is rarely covered in depth in K-12 education, you are correct. The critics, almost all privileged white males such as Ted Cruz, say, "Critical race theory

> Florida is working to create the archetype marshmallow school system statewide. Florida has banned the A.P. Black History, and the A.P. Psychology courses. The course contents offend the dominant white male cultural paradigm.

says every white person is a racist."[5] That statement is the functional equivalent of, "Every true American is a Republican." Neither statement has any connection with reality, but from Cruz's perspective, both are useful lies.

The battle against the CRT strawmen is all about maintaining an educational and schooling focus on the dominant white, male, paradigm. A dozen states, by now perhaps more, have essentially banned the teaching of any alternative paradigm.[6] One state has threatened fines of $1-5 million for "discussions about systemic racism, white privilege, and sexism."[7]

The process that started with Sputnik and the growth of suburbia has continuously undermined American Resilience. The result has been that the American K-12 system has become more and more isolated and independent of the village. The social structures, networks, and systems required to produce and support the development of Resilience have become truncated, less robust, less rich, and less effective.

The present debates about education and schooling demonstrate how weakened and shriveled American Resilience has become. Significant segments of the general population have become fearful of questions and alternative ideas. The lack of questions, and the lack of Resilience has generated a range of mind-boggling stupidities.

- Voting against a school lunch program because students will be spoiled or become addicted.[8]

- Taking horse de-wormer at 50 times the safe dose in lieu of "dangerous" vaccines.

- Wearing a mask becomes a symbol of servitude and weakness on the part of a white male.

- Searching for bamboo slivers in ballots that might have been flown in from China.

The list of these kinds of events over the last two or three years could be continued for several pages. Each of these represents a breakdown of Resilience. And each is connected to, and a product of, the dominant, white male paradigm.

The theme that has been hammered almost to death here is that the complexity and richness of the socio-cultural-ecological system we all live in has been pushed aside, and the connections have been ignored, denied, and broken.

If we look again at the dominant paradigm statement by statement, it becomes even more evident:

- Humans are at the pinnacle, not Nature.

   We start with a short statement that explicitly states that humans are different. They are not part of Nature. Humans are not an integral part of the complexity that is Earth. Every bond between us and the environment is shriveled or broken. The dominant paradigm starts with a statement describing a narrow, dysfunctional vision seeing only a simplified hierarchy.

- There is a natural hierarchy of the fit and unfit; both in humans and Nature.

Again, this divorces humans from Nature. If change is constant, today's perfectly fit are tomorrows unfit. The human hierarchy is totally unnatural. It is man-made and man maintained.

> As for hierarchies of "fitness" in nature, in Nature, consider that the smartest dog makes a really stupid cat while the smartest cat makes a wondrously unintelligent raven.

- The free-willed, self-controlled individual is responsible and sacrosanct.

This might be true on an island with a population of one. Otherwise, this statement contravenes the formal and informal social contracts, such as ethics and laws, constraining the individual. Those contracts are expressions of connections that are denied here. The cliché expression

> Taken to its logical conclusion, the iconic, self-made man is the feral child made good. That will not, cannot, ever happen. There never have been any self-made men.

is "The self-made man." Such a thing cannot exist. It is an oxymoron arising from a denial of the patterns of connection that undergird our lives.

- Human fitness and value can be quantified economically through competition.

Clearly not. It is almost the reverse. Mothers earn zero. Those who build, supply, provide, or serve earn thousands, while those who move paper from one end of the desk to the other earn millions. If we got rid of the CEO's earning millions of dollars, very few of us, maybe none of us, would notice the difference. Let nurses, small scale farmers, firefighters, or waiters all go on strike, and we would all notice the difference immediately. There is virtually no connection between this statement and reality.

- There is always room at the top for one more fit individual.

The operative word here is "fit" which means "just like me." The top layer of the hierarchy is a little bit like a bowl of chili; lots of the same beans steeped for a long time in the preparatory spices, with a little bit of meat thrown in for contrast. Chili can be a work of culinary art. But a diet of all chili, nothing but chili, would lead to dire results. This is a case where the paradigm is willfully blind to the dynamism and complexity of the human condition.

- Newtonian mechanics pretty much rule the visible Universe.

Inherent in Newtonian Mechanics is the assumption of predictability. If initial conditions are known, final conditions can be predicted. This approximation is usefully close to reality for relatively simple conditions. We use it all the time when we enter the crosswalk. But even there, it sometimes fails, and the World is far more complex. Can initial conditions be known sufficiently to make a reliable prediction? No. There is always the unknown fourth, or maybe tenth, place decimal combined with systemic degrees of freedom that creates apparent Chaos. Chaos is not random, but it is unpredictable. The idea the World is Newtonian through and through severs the connections with all the complexity and richness of our Socio-cultural-ecological systems.

- A linear, *post hoc, propter hoc,* reductionist analysis provides effective problem solving.

This is the idea that events occur in a linear fashion of cause and effect. This is an idea derived from Newtonian mechanics. As a starting point, it may have utility but precludes connections to the existent complexities. If event "A" causes event "B" which causes event "C" which causes event "A." Where do "*post*" and "*proptor*" fit? Anywhere,

> The chicken-egg question illustrates an important point. With mutual causality, there is no differential between the two elements. They are both *post* and *propter*.

and everywhere. Wherever you look, the World has these feedback loops leading to mutual causality. Ignoring mutual causality leads to unsuccessful interventions and isolation from the reality of the World.

- A strictly utilitarian commodification of the less-fit and non-human.

Today, it is fashionable to put dollar values on all facets of Nature and ecological services including the cultural services of beauty. In terms of equity, just three recent examples,

- the decades-long battle to put extraction-profits from the Pebble Mine over premier salmon runs,

- the denial of the spiritual significance of the location for the Oak Flat, Rio Tinto copper mine,

> The point to be made is that the costs are driven down the hierarchy while benefits go up. The single most egregious example being the buying and selling of human beings. It certainly does simplify things when a human can be commodified. /s

- the willingness to risk the quality and quantity of fresh water and food for the oil-sands profits generated by the Line 3 pipeline.

In some ways this is the culmination of all that goes before. Here the beneficial connections are going up to support the top levels of the hierarchy. The externalized costs or inequities that have been, are, or would have been, the results of these acts, are somewhere between enormous and incredible. Those inequities would never be borne by the dominant white male culture.

This dominant white male paradigm is pervasive across America. Perhaps most Americans do not buy-into the entire paradigm lock, stock, and barrel because much of it is ludicrous and dehumanizing. However, it remains the dominant paradigm because it absolutely benefits those at the top, or close to the top. Those are the scavengers and the wannabes who have the voice, dollars, influence, and power to push and maintain the paradigm across society.

However, no matter how well it serves the top, according to Strauss and Howe[12], this paradigm is likely on its way out. The paradigm is being overwhelmed by the rate of change and fails to provide Resilience. All paradigms are limited. They cannot provide every answer in every case, every context, or every time. If a paradigm does so, it is no longer a paradigm. It has become an ideology. For a significant part of the American population, the dominant white male paradigm has become an ideology. By their very nature, ideologies preclude anything that might fit the definition of Resilience.

Chapter 5

# How Do We Change Paradigms to Build Resilience?

The question is, if we survive tomorrow, can we rebuild American Resilience to address the extraordinary rate of change coming our way? The answer is yes, we can, but doing so will require creating a story similar to The Miracle on the Hudson. Success will only be possible if there are multiple, perhaps millions of perspectives, of a huge number of people not panicking, and willing to do some heavy lifting. In short, we will need to undergo a massive paradigm shift.

Thomas S. Kuhn published *The Structure of Scientific Revolutions,* in 1970,[1] a book that revamped the way people understood the history of science, and, perhaps, the history of social change and progress. Up until that moment, the history of science was viewed primarily as an accretion of layers of knowledge and understanding. Over time, the process might accelerate. We might be learning more rapidly, but progress was on an accelerating but smooth curve.

Kuhn argued the curve of scientific progress was characterized by periods of gradual, uniform, regular, progress punctuated by revolutionary leaps to new understandings. He termed these leaps paradigm shifts. Each of which would be followed by a period of gradual, uniform, regular progress until the next paradigm shift. The accretion of knowledge was a series of steps rather than a smooth upward slope.

Paradigm shifts do not always arrive with clarion bugle-calls announcing their occurrence. Some are tiny and unrecognized at the time but reverberate over the years. For example, van Leeuwenhoek's microscope, Pasteur's experiments with spontaneous generation, or Mendeleyev's periodic table. Some shifts are huge and quickly recognized as disruptive. They are recognized by the names associated with them: Copernicus, Newton, Darwin, or Hiroshima.

Not all paradigm shifts happen in science and technology. In social structures, examples of paradigm shifts would include, but are not limited to, The Magna Carta, Women's Suffrage, Karl Marx, and Martin Luther King. Examples in the broader culture might include sliced bread and the Big Mac. A paradigm shift can also be intensely personal. A cancer diagnosis might trigger a paradigm shift. However, all paradigm shifts tend to have essentially the same sort of structure, the ubiquitous "S" curve.

The entrance to the curve is triggered by the discovery of events, patterns, or questions that cannot be addressed effectively by the present paradigm. There will be a few folks saying that the anomalies require a new way of doing things, and new ways of seeing the World. They will be a minority and, depending on the circumstances, may be actively attacked, and eliminated.

It has been a long time since the terror of polio. Most people do not remember life before the polio vaccine. It has been even longer since the Spanish Flu pandemic. COVID-19 kicked us into a new paradigm. At the beginning of the curve, we were told it was just like the flu, and would disappear by summer. It wasn't and it hasn't, but the early warnings were ignored, shouted down, and generally the messengers were told to sit down and be quiet.

As stated earlier, we knew the pandemic was coming. Although we had suffered through Polio and AIDS and dodged Ebola, there was hesitation with COVID-19. It took time to collect sufficient evidence to convince people that this was not the flu, and to get the general population closer to the vertical portion of the "S" curve. We are now at a new flatter portion towards the top of the curve. The paradigm about pandemics has changed, but there are still the unconvinced, "flat-earthers," passing state laws to cripple a rapid response to the next pandemic.

These last paragraphs are a good description of the patterns that occur during a paradigm shift. The paradigm shift triggered by COVID-19 was relatively rapid. Most social-cultural paradigm shifts spend more time in the introductory phase. It is difficult to precisely know the moment when the upward curve starts to accelerate. Is it looming just below the horizon?

Over the last twenty years, a series of disparate events and processes have been fraying the dominant social structure paradigm implicit in the "Leave it to Beaver" vision. A couple of examples will suffice.

- 9/11/2001 changed American society. Our confidence took a hit. It turned out that not everybody was enamored with the "city upon the hill." We became uncertain and afraid of our neighbor in ways forgotten since McCarthy.

- In 2008, the culmination of off-shoring and Wall Street speculation was the hollowing out of cities like Detroit and small-town Main Streets. As the economy crashed, it became clear that Wall Street would be bailed out, but there was nothing much for Main Street. The top levels of the hierarchy were protected turf.

- In 2010, *Citizens United* allowed corporations to use bullhorns to drown out the voices of the voters. The vast majority of American information, from radio to books, is now controlled by less than a dozen CEO's. To say nothing about the fact that the Koch brothers, and the Murdochs, knowingly spread lies in support of white supremacy and expend huge resources overwhelming locally funded candidates.

- Concurrent with all these events was the militarization of the police. The Rockwellian vision of a friendly cop on the corner has been replaced by a full-on, occupying force with military grade weaponry that too often seems to function as prosecutor, judge, jury, and executioner.

- In 2016, we installed an administration characterized by unprecedented insularity, immorality, and ignorance about poverty, racism, rankism, environmental degradation, extinction, global heating, food insecurity, and widespread social and economic injustice. In short, it was an administration dead set on cementing into place the dominant white male paradigm. The remnants of that administration are still in Congress, and the leadership is threatening to return in 2024.

- In 2021, forty-three Republican senators voted to excuse an attempted coup, and the Supreme Court morphed into a secretive Star Chamber willing, multiple times, to excuse an attempted legislated and legal coup and to affirm white male supremacy as a facet of the law of the land.

As independent events, this is a disparate list. However, there is a common underlying pattern of protecting the hierarchy by building walls of misinformation and lies to break the patterns of connections that underpin community. The strategy has been to stress *ad nauseum* that the structure of society is the rational result of

- a natural hierarchy of the fit and unfit; both in humans and Nature.

- The free-willed, self-controlled, independent individual is responsible and sacrosanct.

Because most of the public information is controlled by a few white male oligarchs, there is rarely a discussion of the built-in advantages that accrue to the upper layers. The two statements about the natural hierarchy and sacrosanct individual have been repeated, stressed, and legally enhanced such that they are a prime example of an ideology that brooks no compromise. Like all ideologies there are the true believers, i.e., anti-maskers and anti-vaxxers. There are the grifters, i.e., election deniers, governors, and pillow makers. And there is a totemic leader basking in the adulation and sacrifice of the true believers.

And then, there are the wage earners. Once again, the high-income folks get debts of hundreds of thousands, or more, forgiven, but it is a moral issue to forgive college debts. It is fine for the Federal Reserve to decide we need several million unemployed to lower inflation, but we cannot address massive increases in corporate profits or corporate price fixing.[15] The benefits travel up the hierarchy. Costs travel down.

The fact that the contents of these last several paragraphs are generally accepted as true but unfortunate by a significant portion of the American population may indicate that we are approaching an accelerating part of the "S." That the country may be starting a steeper upward slope is indicated by the responses to the George Floyd murder, the summer of BLM protests, the January 6 insurrection, the *Dobbs* decision or to the realization that our former president made the names of our overseas intelligence sources available to any passerby who might find such information lucrative.

These events combined with the dawning recognition that a majority of Republican politicians and candidates will not, in fact cannot, respond effectively, and are a major part of the problem, accelerates the rise of discontent. It may be that we are past the beginning of the more vertical portion of the S curve. If so, there is a high likelihood of a single or series of events causing a paradigm shift, or a crisis, occurring sooner rather than later.

What will the crisis look like? What direction will it come from? There is plenty of material to put together a series of guesses, but truth is any guess is just that, a guess. In any case, no matter what the crisis is, the dominant paradigm will fail as any ideology must fail in the face of the rapid, cataclysmic changes arriving daily.

Is it too late to build Resilience? If the definition of Resilience is the ability to maintain identity and function in the face of change, then the question becomes can the United States of America maintain its identity as striving for the American Idea? The answer is a qualified yes, but success cannot be based solely on schools and schooling.

Schools may be the focus here, but the ideas are equally applicable to the Boy Scouts, Girl Scouts, 4H, FFA, the Lions, the Rotary's, the Kiwanis, and every other civic oriented service club. Radio, TV, newspapers, and magazines must start recognizing and calling out by name the propaganda stream paid for by oligarchs, white supremacists, Christian nationalist, and the GOP, voiced by Fox News *et al* in general and Tucker Carlson wannabes in particular.

The short answer to the question of how to rebuild the power and richness of the American Idea is to re-establish the patterns of connections that undergird our lives, our Resilience, and our ability to thrive. Almost half a century ago, Gregory Bateson built a launching pad for this task with a statement and a question. The statement, "The major problems of the World are the result of the difference between how Nature works, and the way people think."[2]

And the question, "Why do schools teach almost nothing of the pattern which connects? … What's wrong with them? What pattern connects the crab to the lobster and the orchid to the primrose and all four of them to me? And me to you? And all six of us to the amoeba in one direction and to the back-ward schizophrenic in another?"[3]

What Bateson is calling for is a dramatic paradigm shift about how we teach and what we teach. We need to move away from a paradigm where Math is somehow different from French and different from Art or Music, whereas Science is different from History and English literature. Where writing a sentence is in a different universe than skipping rope. What is called for here is a radical revision of Epistemology into a seamless, but not uniform, whole.

There is no more clarion call for the abolition of tunnel vision. Nature is minute and universal. Nature is physical, and not. Nature is patterned and chaotic. Humans and crabs share patterns, and don't. The schizophrenic and the primrose are both natural, with different natures. We could go on and on.

Is there a meta-pattern, or pattern of patterns, here? Can we imagine a paradigm with a sufficient caliber to visualize those kinds of dualities and

> Bateson was far ahead of the curve. It turns out pattern recognition is a fundamental literacy.[4&5]

distinctions? Yes, it would be a kaleidoscope with sufficient diameter to climb through to the end and see the World through an ever-changing translucent lens.

There is a ready-made, readily accessible, panoramic paradigm that provides a foundation for just such a perspective and can be applied to provide a road map about how to do this. The paradigm is The Natural History Approach, and a prime example of its application is The Lewis and Clark Expedition.

The modern Natural History Approach is an outgrowth of Environmentalism. There is a long history of individuals concerned about the degradation of the environment, even before the burning of coal during the late 1800's. In the

United States, the early names associated with this concern include John Muir, and Henry David Thoreau, but the modern movement was triggered by Aldo Leopold's, *A Sand Country Almanac*[6] and the formation of an active Sierra Club.

> In addition to Thoreau and Muir: William Penn required an acre of trees left for every five cleared (1690). Benjamin Franklin fought for clean water, clean air, and waste disposal (1739). Ralph Waldo Emerson wrote about appreciating Nature for itself (1836). Yellowstone National Park was created (1872) and Arbor Day was established the same year.

The next piece of well-known writing was Rachel Carson's *Silent Spring* in 1962[7]. And finally, James Lovelock published *Gaia, A New Look at Life on Earth* in 1979[8]. These people were giants, and, with many others, started to change the American views about the commodification of the less fit, and non-human. Their impact has been massive, but it has yet to cause a pervasive, cultural paradigm shift.

The traditional Natural History Approach has not challenged the dominant reductionist paradigm for two reasons. The first is that each piece of work was idiosyncratic and unique. There could never be a second *Sand Country Almanac* nor a second *Silent Spring*. Individually, they were convincing, but they did not, could not, form a pattern. Second, they were exquisite explanations of "what now" but were not as effective about "what next."

All that has changed with the advent of accessible computers and General Systems Theory. As was pointed out previously, most previous paradigm shifts are associated with an individual. They have a name; Aristotle, Newton, Darwin, Picasso, Jackson Pollock, Einstein, Martin Luther King. This shift is not associated with a person but rather with a machine, the computer.

> Maybe it hasn't changed. As this is written, Alito has trashed the protection of our water supplies from profit making pollution. He continues to privatize the commons for profit. We have just been set back to the time before Nixon. Justice Alito is the poster child for the dominance of ideology over intelligence and understanding.

Natural History has become an interface between the technology of computers and the beauty of Nature. Computers have allowed Natural History to become patterned, replicable, and predictive. It has become a tailor-made paradigm to harness the power of the computer in a humane and regenerative fashion.

Just as the human nervous system cannot handle a sensory overload very well, it cannot handle an analytical overload. We can handle a linear progression such as, "A" causes "B," "B" causes "C" and "C" causes "D." But if we are presented with two statements such as, If "A" then "B," else 50% "C" combined with, If "B" then 24% "A," else "X" or "Y," it becomes very difficult to keep track of things in our head. For example, in words, the previous two sentences might read, "If it rains, we go to the movies; if sunny, we might go to the beach. If sunny, too hot, we go to the movies or perhaps the mall, or we stay home." Given these two sentences, do we know what we are going to do this afternoon? If we were trying to describe a natural system, the complexity quickly outstrips our analytical abilities. Hence, reductionist Science, where we limit the interactions to "A" (may) cause "B."

Do not misunderstand what is being said here. I have oversimplified a bit and the reductionist approach across the breadth of culture is a very powerful tool that essentially carried us from the Neolithic to the present age. However, before the advent of accessible computers, we were limited in our abilities to address the complexities at the edge of Chaos found in Nature. Up to that point, the way we did science was, in part, the result of these limitations on our abilities to think.

The advent of the computer has changed that. Most of us use the computer as a slow telephone, a monster library, an entertainment source, a smart typewriter, a big file cabinet, a camera, and, perhaps, a calculator. Most of us have not yet started to use their unsung abilities of allowing us to think about complex phenomena in ways we have never been able to before.

Instead of being limited to one, two, or a few interactions, the computer allows us to watch, analyze, and deal with a great many interactions between a great many elements. In short, we can begin to simulate and model the behavior of complex systems.

Systems are defined as a set of interacting components structured to produce an outcome or output that no individual component could produce on its own. The components may be material, energy, or information and meaning. Interacting generally means exchanging material or energy. However, interactions may also be predominantly about the exchange of information. i.e., language.

A system must be doing something. If it is not doing something, it is not a system. Right now, you are a system. Think about all the things you are doing right now and all the outcomes or outputs you are creating. If you were to die, all that would cease. You would no longer be a system. Things would still happen, but it wouldn't be you. It would be an entirely different system, still doing some of the same sorts of things but in different ways.

A switch turning on or off a lamp is a simple system. It is a system because the switch has two alternative states: on or off. If it can only be off, it is not a system because it is "not doing anything." Thus, a pile of marbles is not a system in a normal sense because their interactions do not have an on/off switch, nor can they produce an outcome qualitatively different than a single marble. It is an aggregation or a pile.

Another important distinction between an aggregation or a pile and a system is that I can cut or divide a pile of marbles and get two, smaller piles of marbles. Qualitatively nothing changes. You cannot do that to a cow, or to a school, or to an airplane.

A system involving humans may or may not be designed; most human systems have components that just happen. A kitchen may be designed. But it is not a kitchen system until a cook starts interacting with the elements. The outcomes of those interactions cannot be predicted from the physical design; it may be ten kinds of wonderful or ten disasters. A single element, in this case the cook, changes a designed system into a natural system, a generally more complex and unpredictable type of system.

> The Grand Canyon is a system of more than material and energy components. The Paiute Indians called the canyon, the "Mountain Lying Down." The best that the Europeans could come up with was the "Big Canyon." John Wesley Powell created the "Grand Canyon" system in 1871 including the material and energy components plus the nonphysical elements of Human perception, information and meaning.

To restate the definition; a system, designed or natural, is a set of components constantly interacting physically, energetically, informationally, to produce an outcome over time. The outcome, or output, may, or may not, be predicted with a high degree of certainty.

John Muir wrote, "When we try to pick out anything by itself, we find it hitched to everything else in the Universe." Another way of saying the same sort of thing is that there are no isolated "events." There are only patterns. Every event is connected to precursors that were connected, interacting, and existed over time. Viewing any happening or phenomenon as an event in isolation precludes understanding and management.

An example of the traditional science paradigm versus the Systems Paradigm is found in the explanation of the American plague of mass shootings. The traditional, or reductionist, paradigm sees each shooting as an event, isolated and unique, and grants primary causality to idiosyncratic events, mental illness or, equally, to the existence and availability of assault rifles.

> Simple statements: Guns kill people. People kill people. Limit guns for safety. Good guys' guns are safety. Uvalde proves untruth. The Covenant proves truth. But none saves kids.

Each of these components plausibly play a role, but to assert sole causality is fatuous. Mass shootings are the results of a pattern of physical and nonphysical components interacting in a complex fashion to produce an outcome impossible to achieve by a single component. In short, they are the product of a system.

Which brings up a second implication of the Systems Paradigm; a lack of certainty. Very reasonable people can discuss at length what components make up a "mass shooting" system, how those components might interact, and how the system might work to produce the outcome. After all, there are many individuals participating in very similar systems who never carry out a mass shooting. Certainty and prediction are impossible.

Even though thousands and thousands of individuals are enmeshed in a system that might produce a mass shooter, the individual's initial situations or conditions are just different enough that the system produces a different outcome. This is the same phenomenon that allows one child to rise from a socially toxic background to be a mob-boss and another, with apparently the same background, to rise as a world-class poet, or a third who simply finds life untenable and ends it.

While prediction in a particular instance may be uncertain, it is not impossible. In most cases the system can be changed to increase the probability of a desired outcome. We know that is possible. We do it all the time. It is called analysis, planning, and implementation. It also goes by the names of advising, counseling, teaching, and investing. None of these are guaranteed to achieve the ends we want but generally make those ends more likely.

The sensitivity to initial conditions is the result of compounding probabilistic interactions. If a difference in initial conditions changes the probabilities of initial interactions, those changes may reverberate throughout the system. The fact that each interaction has a finite range of possibilities means that the outcome must also have a finite range of possibilities. If you plant corn, you will get more or less corn, but you will not get wheat. If you cut your workers' salaries, you might get a strike, or sabotage, or acquiescence, but you are unlikely to get bouquets of roses.

The third major implication of the Systems Paradigm is that the World is metaphorically flat. Man loses his position at the top of the pyramid. As an example of what "flat" means, consider the traditional scope of Biology. That scope could be broken down in many ways, but commonly, the big three are Botany, Zoology, and Ecology; none of which traditionally seriously consider Humans as their purview.

Humans are the focus of Anatomy and Physiology. As such there has traditionally been a disciplinary boundary between squirrels and humans; between the temperate forest community and the urban neighborhood. You couldn't study them the same way; people were special. You could not, as a friend suggested, simply consider a medical doctor an overspecialized veterinarian. They were different.

Within the Systems Paradigm, those distinctions and boundaries between humans and the rest become so porous as to be nonexistent. The contents and events may seem to be unique, but the underlying patterns are very much the same. We are not *Primus enter pares*, we are *Pares enter pares*. We are precisely subject to the laws, rules, constraints, and boundaries that determine the limits of the rest of the Universe. We are not lords above all. We are, and must be, a part of the system.

If all this seems familiar, common sense, and generally accepted, it is because a great many people have been thinking, talking, and writing in this way for a good while. As a result, some of the vocabulary has entered the

> *Urban Dynamics* by Jay Forrester, 1969, mapped out an entire field of research and application based on System Dynamics in social systems. The results of which remain germane today.[17]

daily language. Can you get through a day without reading or hearing somewhere, somehow, about systems, inputs, outputs, feedbacks, or tipping points? The vocabulary is pervasive but is used without really connecting to a shift in understanding how the World works.

Classic examples are the efforts by Presidents Bush and Obama, with the enthusiastic support of the Gates, the Broad, and the Walton foundations, amongst others, to reform education based on a business model. The reforms include:

- reliance on competition and free-market strategies to cut costs, including salaries,

- more freedom to fire principals and teachers, and more closing of low-scoring schools.

- instituting merit pay based on equations based on some phantasmagorical model rather than observations.

A fitting metaphor for this kind of corporate-school model is a factory filling cereal boxes. As the boxes move through the production line, they go through quality control stations. If they are found to be smudged or light weight, they are pushed off; perhaps to be recycled, or perhaps discarded. Everybody and everything have a place and are woven into a very orderly and efficient pattern; outputs and "profits" are maximized.

This is a great model of a schooling process. It is an elegant description of a path forward. Unfortunately, this model has one glaring and fatal omission based on a failure to understand system dynamics. It focuses on the system's output. It does not acknowledge the system's input. With the possible exceptions of the military boot camps and hospitals, no other social system, and certainly no corporate system, deals with the variety of inputs that come to the school door on a daily basis.

Boot camps address the variety of inputs in a number of effective ways that are probably unacceptable in the majority of schools. Hospitals deal with the variety by limiting the measures of success, live or die, and by having potentially high expenditures. When a model of a school system ignores the potential variety of inputs, everything else about the model is suspect, and potentially misleading and destructive. The application of the systems concepts and vocabulary to any complex issue needs to grow out of a fuller understanding of the actual paradigm.

The formal Systems Paradigm was initially developed starting in the 1940s; in part as a response to the need to control anti-aircraft guns during World War 2. Ludwig Von Bertalanffy wrote *General Systems Theory* (1968)[10] and Ross Ashby wrote, *Introduction to Cybernetics* (1956)[11]. The former is a more general treatment and is generally considered the founding document of the modern Systems Paradigm. The latter is focused more on engineering and control.

> Inputs to complex systems are important. A teenager went blind on a diet of white, i.e., potato chips, french-fries', white bread, and a bit of pork.[9] Book banners and curriculum monitors beware.

In the past fifty years, the Systems Paradigm has undergone rapid development in a disparate range of sciences and social sciences. However, the core of the paradigm has maintained a constant and coherent focus,

- on holism rather than particularism,

- on linkages / interactions rather than components,

- on patterns rather than events,

- on emergent structures and functions,

- on output as a product of system structure and function, rather than environment

> In General Systems Theory, common patterns frequently found in ongoing systems are referred to as generic structures. We tend to learn by pattern recognition. "Pattern recognition can lead to new discoveries, breakthrough ideas, and innovative concepts."[12]

- and on uncertainty when dealing with complex, stochastic systems.

A more detailed explanation of the Systems Paradigm would include the following axioms:

1.  Analysis and synthesis must be present.

    The Systems Paradigm demands both be done simultaneously. Analysis allows identification of system components; synthesis identifies the connections and interactions. The identity of the system does not lie so much in the nature of the components. The identity of the system is primarily found in the nature of the interactions and connections.

    > Consider the differences between a high school classroom and the same function down the street at Juvie. The components may be similar, but the connections tend to be different, and the outputs are not the same.

2.  The structure of a system determines how the system functions or behaves.

    The effect of the system's environment is indirect and does not generally determine the system output. To change the system's behavior, change the system including acceptable inputs. Do not bother wrestling with the environment.

The net result of these first two axioms is that the Systems Paradigm is holistic rather than reductionist. To analyze, understand, and manage a system, you need to look at the details of the interactions and while keeping the overall pattern in view. To understand the action of one component or interaction, it is necessary to understand the patterns surrounding it. One interaction or one component is rarely if ever, going to determine the output of any but the simplest system.

3.  Every system contains subsystems and is a subsystem of yet a larger system.

> *Great fleas have little fleas upon their backs to bite 'em,*
> *And little fleas have lesser fleas, and so ad infinitum.*
> *And the great fleas themselves, in turn, have greater fleas to go on;*
> *While these again have greater still, and greater still, and so on.*
> *Augustus De Morgan, in "A Budget of Paradoxes"[13]*

The inputs to any system are the outputs of other systems. The outputs of any system will be the inputs to another system.

4.  Systems vary in their complexity.

There are four broad patterns of behavioral complexity.

a)  The deterministic pattern is generally structurally simple. The classic example is a limited thermostat - furnace system. A change in environmental input, temperature, triggers an "on" or "off" change in the system. It either produces heat or it doesn't, not much variety. One can learn about this sort of system function using trial and error.

b)  In the moderately stochastic class of systems, a change in input triggers a quantitative change in output. An example of this sort of system might be a cornfield. The components in the corn field system include, but are not limited to, field preparation, soil contents precipitation air temperature, insolation, and corn variety. Any one of which might vary in what inputs they bring to the system. However, whatever the variation, the output is more corn or less corn. A cornfield does not suddenly produce alfalfa. This sort of system can be described in terms of statistics.

> A baseball game is similar to the corn field, if the rules are followed. The output is always "runs." Break the rules and a new system is created. Maybe its cricket, maybe its "Calvinball," or maybe it's a brawl, but it isn't baseball.

c)  A severely stochastic system is one where a change in input may bring about a limited number of qualitative changes in output. If the manager of a shoe factory decides to cut wages, the output might be no change, a drop in production, or quality, or sabotage, or a strike. However, the number of probable qualitative changes is limited. There will not be a bouquet of flowers, and each of the likely outputs can be assigned a probability. This level of complexity can be described using a series of Boolean expressions of the format, If "this" then "that," else "those." A short series of these kinds of expressions quickly outstrips our ability to predict a particular outcome in any specific instance.

> Four years of college is this system. There are numerous unnamed outcomes with tiny probabilities. There is a limited number of named outcomes, each of which has a significant probability of happening.

d)  The most analytically complex type of system is indeterminate. These are complicated systems that contain unknown, perhaps invisible, elements, connected with high degrees of freedom. A small change in inputs to such a system may generate such a broad range in output that no significant probability can be assigned to any particular output. The classic example here would be evolution of a complex biotic community or the changes in long-term social development. Why do two children seemingly raised in identical conditions turn out so differently? These are analytically intractable systems. The only approach is to use intuition. Of course, intuition is often wrong, but if it is used appropriately, it is being used only with the most difficult complex, and unpredictable situations. Therefore, intuition is often legitimately incorrect.

> Intuition is "an experiential system because its primary function is to learn from experience. It operates in a manner that is associative, preconscious, automatic, nonverbal, imagistic, rapid, effortless, concrete, holistic, intimately associated with affect, intrinsically highly compelling, and minimally demanding of cognitive resources."[14]

The way we approach analyze, understand, and manage a natural system must respond to the nature of the system. Too often severely stochastic social issues are addressed and managed using approaches based on statistics appropriate to a less complex type of system. Failure to understand and manage is the result. For example, if you wished to lower the local crime rate, however defined, should you,

- arrest and jail corner level drug dealers?

- arrest and confine local level users?

- increase surveillance and patrols?

- focus on the pill makers and international cartels?

- spend resources on reduction and amelioration of addiction through locally recruited NGO's, influencers, programs, and supports?

- do some locally determined combination of all the above and more using tax dollars?

Experience does not leave any doubt that the drug addiction-crime nexus is a wicked problem, and no single approach will solve the problem. For that reason, using any statistics based on one or more actions as the measure of success is probably a mistake, and will paint an inaccurate picture of success or failure.

5.  Complex systems do not behave in a linear fashion.

    Complex systems are unlikely to function in a linear fashion. Doubling the input does not always result in doubling the output; nor does halving the input always halve the output. Complex systems often have mutually causal components where "A" causes "B" and "B" directly, or indirectly, causes "A." Once the system is kicked by a change of inputs, any number of reinforcing relationships may be triggered to compound or counteract the effect.

    In every system, there will always be a delay between the change in input and a change in output. In a simple, deterministic system, the delay may be very short. In a large, severely stochastic system, e.g., the Earth's ecosystem, the delay may be hundreds or thousands of years or longer.

    A second source of delay in a stochastic system is the system adapting to change. In complex systems, some, perhaps most, interactions and connections can be altered to some degree. What this means is a change occurs in an interaction to absorb a change in input such that the output does not change. A friendship is an example of a complex adaptive system that can withstand a broad range of input changes without altering the friendship.

There may come a point where a change in input finally exceeds the ability to adapt. If one or more interactions can no longer absorb the change, they break or change dramatically. When this happens, the system structure or function will rapidly change, and the output is likely to radically change. This is the famous "tipping point."

> Winning the lottery is often a catastrophe from which the winner may never recover. Sometimes this happens in social and political systems: The Pettus Bridge, The Stonewall Inn, and, perhaps, George Floyd.

A catastrophe is defined as a radical change in a context. At a tipping point, a tiny change of input catastrophically changes output. This is not about a modification of the extant system. A tipping point essentially destroys the previous system and replaces it with a new system. It is a new set of relationships.

The thing about tipping points is that they are often impossible to predict. Catastrophes are generally a surprise. For instance, a best-friend may stick with their best-friend through all sorts of disagreements, slights, or difficulties, but totally end the relationship over a tiny, almost invisible event. Or consider a mistreated dog. If you approach the dog with a stick, it may back up into a corner and cower. You stop moving, the dog cowers, and then suddenly attacks. What changed? What triggered the radical shift? The same happens sometimes in a bullying situation. The victim may acquiesce over and over. And then suddenly; the victim answers back with more or less violence.

6.   Complex systems are self-organizing.

Change is constant. Any complex system that exists over time must adapt to change. The ability to adapt to change is a function of feedback where a system output connects with, and modifies, a system input or process. A familiar description would be "I am hungry, I eat, I am full, I stop eating." The output or process being monitored does not have to be the final one. The ratio of dollar-expenditure rates over income rates or the governor on a steam engine are components or processes generally buried somewhere in the center of a system and responding to the behavior of the system as a whole. This is the same kind of process that any system uses to "learn" about its performance.

One other aspect of self-organization is the possibility of the emergence of a behavior, or output that cannot be predicted by looking at the components or a previous state of the system. The classic example of emergence is the existence of life. There is no cellular component or structure that in and of itself predicts the existence of life. It is all those components, all those interactions, all that complexity that generates life.

On a less exotic level, with the greatest skills and best management, is there an experienced teacher willing to predict with certainty in September how their class will function in June? What will be the corporate culture? Certainly, as part of the classroom system, the teacher's input shapes the outcome but is not controlling. The specific outcome is the result of hundreds of daily decisions made by parents, students, other teachers, and administrators, on the fly, with little reflection, and, most often, quickly forgotten. Because classrooms can generally be viewed as severely stochastic systems, the outcomes in June will be uniquely detailed, but will generally fall within a normal range for that school. Predictions can play the percentages but not the certainties.

> In 1997, with the merger with McDonnell Douglas, who would have predicted the state of affairs for Boeing in 2024?

7. All systems have two structural traits in common.

All systems have a boundary. It may be a physical structure, the edge of a pond, the shell of an egg, the classroom walls, the skin of a human. It may be a linguistic convenience: headquarters vs. the field, eighth grade vs high school, organic vs inorganic chemistry. A boundary might be created functionally, production vs sales, English vs Spanish or French, athletic department vs the theater group. Or a boundary might just be a cultural or social sense of identity; an "us versus them."

In all cases, the boundary keeps the insides in and the outsides out. In every case, the perceptual and analytical boundaries may be somewhat arbitrary. You may study the family dynamics but ignore the community. You may study the pond but not the surrounding forest. These boundaries may make sense, but they are still to some degree arbitrary.

Every boundary must be porous to some degree. The Laws of Thermodynamics preclude isolated, self-contained systems. Systems constantly do something; or they are not a system. Doing something always requires energy, and often material, and information. Therefore, the selectively porous boundary is an important function for system maintenance and identity.

Every cultural or social system has boundaries, and has a recruiting and initiation process that determines, along with

> The isolated, developing chick needs oxygen coming across the shell. Even its distant cousins, turtles and crocodilians, must leave their eggs in air, not water, for available oxygen.

ascribed characteristics, who becomes a member and who will not. Ascribed characteristics might include, but not be limited to, gender, race, age, income, familial ties and descent, belief systems, and on and on. All those stereotypes we use to define strangers are ascribed characteristics. The fundamental ascription that is searched for is, "They are just like us."

The schooling, training, or initiation is a preparation for convincing gatekeepers that the neophyte is worthy and, despite some minor differences, is indeed "just like us." Of course, nobody is just like us, so the gatekeepers must walk a very fine line. They must be flexible enough to, at a minimum, replace group losses or, perhaps, grow the group. On the other hand, they must be strict enough that the group identity is not diluted or lost.

Despite their importance, it is not always clear exactly who the gatekeepers are. Sometimes, they are the folks out front, the teachers, trainers or initiators, but frequently, they are the folks we never see, who, in one way or another, underwrite and protect the system's functions. Examples might include bank red-liners, university admission committees, golf club membership committees.

A second structural trait common to all systems, but most evident in social systems, is a three-phase life cycle; for lack of better terminology, a juvenile, a mature, and a senescent phase.

- Juvenile systems use most of their energy, material, and information resources to develop, establish, and perhaps expand both implicit and explicit structure; fewer resources are used to produce an output. This is a period of establishing structure, including connections, interactions, and identifying initial conditions, inputs and goals or outputs.

- Mature systems expend most of their resources on producing output with fewer resources used for maintenance. This will be a period where the system rolls along doing as expected with minimum time and effort spent on system maintenance. These are the systems just humming along, doing their job efficiently and well; able to absorb the vagaries coming their way with little effort.

- Senescent systems reduce resources consumed in production and increase resources used for maintenance. This is a period of withdrawal and dissolution of the system. Often, there is an effort to re-establish a new system; an exchange of contact information, promises to get together, and affirmations that "This was good."

  The life cycle is not divided into thirds. The duration of any phase is highly variable. And any phase can be interrupted or triggered by changes in the components, environment, or input. A corollary is that all social systems, and most natural systems, must constantly spend resources on maintenance. A purely task oriented social system will be brittle, but a system focused solely on maintenance will be ineffective. Both situations will lead to dissolution.

These seven axioms portray a very different approach to the understanding of both natural and social systems. This is a new paradigm. It does not supplant the traditional reductionist science paradigm. The new paradigm functions in the same way pre-relativity / Newtonian Mechanics and post-relativity / Quantum Mechanics answer separate kinds of questions, sometimes together and sometimes apart.

What this new paradigm does is simply shred the dominant, white, male, American ideology. The rational weakness of the paradigm has previously been described, but with the new Systems Paradigm, it cannot even be discussed. The concepts are incommensurate with the systems paradigm. For example,

- Humans are at the pinnacle, not Nature.

  Pinnacle? Really? Where is the pinnacle in any system? Consider your body as a system made up of the usual subsystems. What subsystem could we remove? Pick any one, and death follows sooner rather than later. The same is true of the larger Earth systems and the smaller environmental systems. In every case, it may be possible to remove a subsystem, perhaps by extinction, and have the larger system limp along for a while, but death and replacement is inevitable. There are no pinnacles in natural systems. It is a flat world.

- There is a natural hierarchy of the fit and unfit; both in humans and Nature.

There is no natural hierarchy. The second issue about fit and unfit is a question of congruence. Congruence is only an issue in designed systems. As a ludicrous example, one would not build balsa wood wing struts for a 747. That would be wildly incongruent, but that incongruence could never exist in a natural system. For a natural system to exist, congruency exists from the start. The use of "fit" and "unfit" can only be used this way in a human designed system. There is nothing natural about it, and congruence is totally artificial, man-made, and protectionary.

- The free-willed, self-controlled, independent individual is responsible and sacrosanct.

If a free-willed, self-controlled, independent person exercises free-will, and independence in some unsanctioned manner, one or two things happen. The first is that the rogue becomes isolated and required inputs are reduced or cut entirely. A reduction of inputs equals a reduction in functioning or possibly death and dissolution. A second response is to isolate the rogue and stop processing the system's outputs. The outputs of any system are thermodynamically toxic to that

> Consider a steel mill where steel was never removed. At some point, piles of steel would block deliveries of energy, materials, and information.

system. The outputs must be processed or removed by another subsystem, or death follows. It does not matter whether the output is considered a product or a waste, it will, in time, be toxic. The outputs of a rogue subsystem are difficult to process and likely toxic to the larger system unless contained or isolated.

What looks like unsanctioned independence for the individual is actually the death throes of a subsystem. There is a lack of connection, a cut-off of inputs, a buildup of toxic output, and a concurrent loss of function. Name it: sidewalk mental illness, mass shooter, January 6, or the Unabomber, it is all the same pattern.

- Human fitness and value can be quantified economically through competition.

Natural systems compete, generally for short periods, over temporarily limited resources, and generally without loss of life or function. Natural systems need an ongoing source of hard-earned energy. The death of a male beta wolf, with the loss of all that invested and stored energy, would be an extraordinary waste. Competitive death by error happens; death by intention almost never. A system full of competitive subsystems will not survive for long, nor will the subsystems.

Cooperation wins the day, every day, all day, and that is what is found within and between natural systems. Cooperation, or symbiosis, takes a variety of forms, from parasitism to predation, but is always long-term rather than short-term. This portion of the cultural paradigm about social competition is a bastardization of Social Darwinism. You would be hard pressed to find a paradigmatic statement more incorrect than this one.

- There is always room at the top for one more fit individual, assuming certain social qualifications.

Why keep beating a dead horse? There is no pinnacle or top. Fitness is an artificial construction of human systems designed to limit and protect the throne of privilege.

- Newtonian mechanics pretty much rules the visible Universe.

This statement is true in a limited fashion about the visible, physical Universe, Newtonian Mechanics is of very limited utility for dealing with physical or social system complexities that operate at the edge of Chaos, i.e., most of the natural World.

- A linear, *post hoc, propter hoc,* reductionist analysis provides effective problem solving.

There may be a limited number of examples of linear outputs for deterministic systems, but those are rare, and mostly human designed, systems. Most of the World operates with a degree of stochasticity compounded by multiple feedback loops where "before" and "after" pictures are blurred and irreducible.

- A strictly utilitarian, low value, commodification of the less-fit and non-human makes sense.

In a flat world, if the system has value, then the subsystems are of equal value. How would you commodify the heart over the liver or kidneys? Humans and the Earth systems form a complex system. If we continue to make decisions about the changes coming our way based on the old reductionistic paradigm, more of the connections will fail between subsystems. The systems will fail. New systems will form but the process will be catastrophic and a potential Armageddon.

The dominant, white, male American cultural paradigm has never been able to address the complicated, complex, dynamic condition of the World. At its core, the dominant paradigm has a single, central answer, in multiple guises, to every complex cultural, social, economic, and ecological issue, the protection of ongoing privatization of the commons. "Three centuries of transforming commons into capital have weakened governments and the public interest, allowing dominance by strong corporate actors," [16 p118] "structurally incapable of generosity or ethical behavior."[16 p125]

As the dominant paradigm has devolved into an ideology, it has become toxic to the development of resiliency. Is it even possible to think about, and manage, the changes required by issues such as global warming, or poverty and equity, using this ideology? The evidence is mounting every day that it is not. If not, what might be a more appropriate paradigm?

# Chapter 6

# The Resiliency Paradigm and Thrivancy Education

The Natural History Paradigm is predicated on a sense of wonder. It is not just a childlike sense of wonder because it is not about age. It is about a lack of theoretical constraints, expectations, or presuppositions. An excellent model of this approach is the Lewis and Clark expedition. Although Meriwether Lewis had some military experience, he was not selected to lead on that basis. Rather, President Thomas Jefferson selected Lewis because he could lay claim "to a compleat (sic) science in botany, natural history, mineralogy & astronomy, joined the firmness of constitution & character, prudence, habits adapted to the woods, & a familiarity with the Indian manners & character, requisite for this undertaking."[1]

If you add on top of this the general commission to describe the geography, resources, and rivers of the region to lay claim to the area, you have a mandate to go, look around, connect, and find patterns. After all, Lewis and Clark were not going out into the unknown. All kinds of people had gone before, either by land or by sea. Lewis and Clark were to fill in a picture where the frame was already established.

> Clark had been Lewis' commanding officer in the Army and out-ranked Lewis, but Lewis was in charge. They resolved the issue by addressing each other as "Captain."

Therefore, they certainly had some presuppositions. But their mandate was to claim the land and to buttress that claim with information based on wandering, observing, and documenting the unique, and to connect it all into a compelling narrative capturing the components, connections, and context.

In short, it may have been formalized, but they were just like children going into a large backyard to see what's there today and maybe see something new or something

> Jefferson's instructions to Lewis go on for page after page, but can be boiled down to, "Go, look around, describe everything you see, keep good notes, be kind, and come back safely."[1]

old in a new way. And that is the essence of an approach based on the Natural History Paradigm. To wit,

- An expectation of the new in the exploration of the known,
- An exploration of patterns based on the details of connections,
- Pan-disciplinary,
- Characterized by experience rather than theory,
- Opportunistic in the paths taken to understanding,
- Documented to be available to others.
- Recognition of the importance of observer as part of the observed,

Although Lewis and Clark had a very broad and diffuse mandate for their expedition with few predetermined limits and structural boundaries, they had to go West; not East, not South, and not North. They were limited by time; extensive delays were not acceptable, and they could not have an army. Did the Lewis and Clark Expedition answer all the questions about the Pacific Northwest? Clearly not. But they certainly built a foundation for what came after.

What came after was more Natural History combined with the more usual Reductionist Science Paradigm. The application of the Natural History Paradigm is an extraordinarily powerful exploration of the natural and social World, including systems of wicked problems and systems operating on the edge of Chaos. But it cannot be the totality of the exploration.

It is a question of completeness. Once we have achieved and explored the Natural History approach, or perspective, focused on wholeness and connectivity, the traditional reductionist paradigm is a way to look at individual connections. Absent the Natural History perspective, the traditional approach lacks context and complexity. Without context, there can be little or no meaning. Absent the reductionist approach, the Natural History perspective will lack details, predictive utility, and is unlikely to be a useful tool for change.

The real power of the Natural History Paradigm becomes apparent when it is combined with the more structured Systems Paradigm. The Systems Paradigm describes the structure of both the natural and social world. The Natural History Paradigm is a less technical and more user-friendly approach for exploring that World and thereby provides a bridge between the sometimes abstruse, technical perspective and the more humane way of knowing.

The preservation and continued existence of the American idea requires a melding of these paradigms. The Systems Paradigm depends on the recognition of connections and patterns. The Natural History Paradigm requires exploration and openness to experience. Both allow the incorporation of the Reductionist Paradigm to confirm the contents and reality of connections.

The combination of Natural History, Systems, and Reductionist Paradigms provides a solid foundation for creating, nurturing, and supporting the development of effective responses to the breadth and complexity of the World. In short, this combination supports the development of a Resilience that can maintain function and identity in response to the oncoming changes. Therefore, this combination of paradigms might properly be called the "Resiliency Paradigm."

An advantage of this Resiliency Paradigm is that the approach itself is inherently resilient. Consider for a moment how this paradigm considers the wicked problem of poverty. Just as Natural History recognizes a wide variety of organisms as mammals, the paradigm can recognize a wide variety of contexts and instances of poverty, while the Systems perspective requires examination of the common patterns, inputs, outputs, boundaries, and processes. There is no "one size fits all" here, and in fact, the Resiliency Paradigm would not, indeed could not, be crippled by the discovery and description of new instances or types of poverty. The patterns might be similar but somewhat variable, while the contents were significantly different.

If we were looking at the World through the lens of the Resiliency Paradigm, the possibility of the fantastical, delusional, untethered, paradigms created by the lying for dollars contingent would be reduced or eliminated. The dominant white male ideology would be shown up for the sham it is, and the oligarchs would be held at bay. The crucial question becomes, is it possible to weave this sort of Resiliency Paradigm into the American cultural fabric in time to save the American Idea?

It may be possible. There are signs that the dominant ideology may be fraying around the edges as the decay of the Republican Party is coming to a crisis. The leader of the Party, Donald Trump, just called for "the termination of all rules, regulations, and articles, even those found in the Constitution."[2] While most Republican officials could not find their way to condemn the call, only a few seemed to support it.

Certainly, the recent behavior of the politicized and venal Supreme Court has put the issues right out front where the issues and the dangers are far more explicit and recognizable. Every day brings new headlines about a Supreme Court bought and sold on the open market. Every day, we hear more stories of the five dysfunctional families in the House; each trying to outdo the others in recalcitrance. Every day, more kids are killed, either by police or other kids using the guns of war.

But there are signs of hope; voters fighting back, lawsuits being won, lawsuits thrown out, and daily headlines mocking the lies, prevarications, and ineptitudes of the small-bore politicians. The results of the 2023 election were another speed-bump on the road to crisis. If the dogs in the manger can be held at bay for one or two more election cycles, hope springs eternal, and we may get it done. The Resiliency Paradigm provides a map for using schools and schooling to build resiliency, rebuild social networks, and reaffirm the American Idea now and not just in the future.

We can, indeed we must, build a new education system based on the Resiliency Paradigm to engender Resilience across generations as we face a tsunami of change. To reiterate what has already been said, today, the United States of America is facing an accelerating freight train of change coming straight at us. The name of the train is The Climate Change Express.

> The global cost of climate change is about $16 million per hour.[3]

The freight is loaded in cars with labels including, but not limited to, technology, demographics, agriculture, food and water, migration, and health. The heaviest cars are loaded with socio-economic, ethnographic, racial, gender, and geographic inequities, i.e., externalized costs generated by the changes carried in the other cars.

The dominant, white, male cultural paradigm in America demands inequity and survives solely on the subsidies provided by other people, species, and Earth systems. The inequities will bankrupt the system, sooner rather than later because benefits flow up with little or no return benefit.

More importantly, the dominant paradigm has devolved into an ideology. Paradigms are inherently limited. Resilience demands the ability to shift paradigms as needed. If what we are doing is not working or if what we are doing is actually doing harm, then we must shift to a different paradigm. No paradigm provides all the answers all the time in every circumstance. When a paradigm provides every answer all the time in every circumstance, it is no longer a paradigm. It has become an ideology, and Resilience goes to essentially zero.

At this moment in time, the American Idea is in danger because we do not have the cast of social and cultural paradigms to generate the range of perspectives, approaches, understandings, or tools to effectively address these changes without losing our identity. All the potential Resilience is missing because we have allowed the dominant paradigm to drive other cultural paradigms to the edge, as it were, to beyond the pale.

> There is increasing on-line chatter about Trump becoming a "Red Caesar"[4] or dictator for a day, or getting rid of the 22nd Amendment.

Thousands of answers are out there. We must create opportunities for the upcoming generations to find and re-integrate those paradigms into a more diverse and colorful American Cultural paradigm. For the American Idea to survive, we must start exploring alternative paradigms via a Thrivancy Education incorporating the Resiliency Paradigm.

Is it possible to build an education system that incorporates the Resiliency Paradigm at a foundational level? The answer is yes, but not on a large scale right now. We are too tied to the idea that high stakes tests mean something. We are too enamored with the industrial model of schools where students are like cereal boxes to be filled, weighed, and perhaps discarded. Nor do we really wish to pay teachers the kinds of salaries needed to support the creativity, study, commitment, and hours needed to make such a system work. Perhaps most importantly, the creation of a Thrivancy Education will likely meet full-on resistance from those working to privatize the educational commons.

The industrial model of education and schooling builds on the core of the dominant paradigm, the privatization of the commons. The creation of a public system of education brought education into the realm of the civil commons: "co-operative human constructs that protect and/or enable universal access to life goods."[17] There have always been independent, non-public schools supported by individual or corporate funding. That is not the issue here. The issue here is using public funding to privatize the commons at an accelerating rate.[18]

A prime example is the Arizona Empowerment Scholarship Program which makes public funding available to any student for a wide range of schooling including, but not limited to, home, independent, profit-driven charter, church or parochial, and finally, public school. Along with this program goes a lack of regulation or oversight, with primary benefits to those who already have, a denial of service to those in need, and the opportunity to make a handsome profit.

However, just as some schools are constantly working to move away from the text-centric or test-centric models, individual schools, grade teams, or individual teachers could always push in this new direction. There are always teachers and administrators willing to risk a new path as long as it remains low profile. For those willing to try, there is a solid foundation and launching pad called EL Education, developed by Outward Bound and the Harvard School of Education. This approach has been around since 1991 and has consistently demonstrated success in K-12 schooling.[5]

> Expeditionary learning (EL) programs incorporate many of the features of Lewis and Clark; not everybody follows the same path, nobody is left behind, but learning is an active exploration in depth over time.

A description of EL Education includes the following imperatives.

- Self-discovery, including self-confidence and self-knowledge, both inside and outside of the classroom.

- Having time to look, having time to see, and having time to reflect.

- That learning is both private and corporate.

- Both success and failure, in the presence of compassion and trust, can teach.

- The standard to excel is your past performance.

- Cooperation and compassion are moral imperatives rather than a cost.

- Guidance by the complexity, diversity, and inclusiveness of Nature is a benefit.

- Periodic silence and stillness tie everything together.

This is a program with a deep and broad history of innovation and application that has been very successful on a broad set of measures, personal, social, and academic, including college success. This is also a program that is almost a precise mirror of an education based on the Natural History Paradigm.

There is yet a third approach to education worthy of consideration. In 2004, Robert Fulghum re-wrote the classic, *All I Really Needed to Know, I learned in Kindergarten* (1988)[6]. What he really needed to know can be summarized as:

- Share everything.

- Play fair.

- Don't hit people.

- Put things back where you found them.

- CLEAN UP YOUR OWN MESS.

- Don't take things that aren't yours.

- Say you're SORRY when you HURT somebody.

- Wash your hands before you eat.

- Flush.

- Warm cookies and cold milk are good for you.

- Live a balanced life - learn some and drink some and draw some and paint some and sing and dance and play and work every day some.

- Take a nap every afternoon.

- When you go out into the world, watch out for traffic, hold hands, and stick together.

- Be aware of wonder. Remember the little seed in the Styrofoam cup: The roots go down and the plant goes up and nobody really knows how or why, but we are all like that.

- Goldfish and hamster and white mice and even the little seed in the Styrofoam cup - they all die. So do we.

- And then remember the Dick-and-Jane books and the first word you learned - the biggest word of all - LOOK."

> This is not a technical education. This is about ethics, empathy, and community. The World would be a more humane place if several Justices and the scavenger oligarchs had not forgotten what they could have, and should have, learned in kindergarten.

Consider how this list of important lessons supports the structuring, development, and performance of the system that creates Resilience. Compare that performance to the performance of California's content standards, "which are designed to encourage the highest achievement of every student by defining the knowledge, concepts, and skills that students should acquire at each grade level, and are available for the core subjects at all grade levels, including kindergarten."[7]

> A New York City joke suggests going to a particular kindergarten pretty much determines acceptance to a particular set of universities. Apocryphal? Maybe, but twenty or so private kindergartens divvy up applicants according to "best fit" based on test results, for preschoolers.[8] If entrance to kindergarten is based in part on preparation in pre-K, shouldn't pre-K teachers be paid as well as other teachers because a good pre-K experience apparently makes a difference all the way through high school and college?

One approach supports the system, and the other hobbles it. One expands, and one limits. One suggests multiple paradigms exist side by side. The other defines and limits, acceptable knowledge, concepts, and skills each child must have.

As students age through the school system, the standards become more and more explicit and defined. However, it is understood that the same standards in two classes, with different students, different teachers, and equal but different resources can produce different experiences. Excellent teachers, the master teachers, kind of wave at the standards as they drive by. Standards never set "the high bar." Standards are always the lowest acceptable level. No matter how physically, socially, or intellectually challenging a classroom context may be, it is unlikely that a master teacher sets a goal of 'minimally acceptable." Any school system boasting about "standards" is struggling to achieve the minimum.

The three approaches to learning, EL, Kindergarten, and the Natural History approach, have three different sources, perspectives, vocabularies, and styles. However, the three approaches are coherently able to build upon and expand each other as a basis of Thrivancy Education.

A braid of the three approaches using the following symbols might look like this:

- EL Education
    o The Natural History Approach
        ▪ Everything Learned in Kindergarten

To wit;

- Self-discovery, including self-confidence and self-knowledge, both inside and outside of the classroom.
    o An expectation of new in the exploration of known.
    o Recognition of the importance of observer as part of the observed.
    o Opportunistic in the paths taken to understanding.
        ▪ And then remember the Dick-and-Jane books and the first word you learned - the biggest word of all - LOOK."
        ▪ Live a balanced life - learn some and drink some and draw some and paint some and sing and dance and play and work every day some.
- Having time to look, having time to see, and having time to reflect.
        ▪ And then remember the Dick-and-Jane books and the first word you learned - the biggest word of all - LOOK."
        ▪ Take a nap every afternoon.
        ▪ Warm cookies and cold milk are good for you.

- That learning is both private and corporate.
  - o An exploration of patterns based on details of connections,
  - o And documented, available to others.
    - ▪ Share everything.
    - ▪ When you go out into the world, watch out for traffic, hold hands, and stick together.
- Both success and failure, in the presence of compassion and trust, can teach.
  - o An expectation of new in the exploration of known.
- The standard to beat is your past performance.
  - o An expectation of new in the exploration of known.
  - o Opportunistic in the paths taken to understanding.
    - ▪ Play fair.
    - ▪ Put things back where you found them.
    - ▪ CLEAN UP YOUR OWN MESS.
    - ▪ Say you're SORRY when you HURT somebody.
- Cooperation and compassion are moral imperatives rather than a cost.
  - o Recognition of the importance of observer as part of the observed.
    - ▪ Share everything.
    - ▪ Play fair.
    - ▪ Put things back where you found them.
    - ▪ CLEAN UP YOUR OWN MESS.
    - ▪ Say you're SORRY when you HURT somebody.
    - ▪ When you go out into the world, watch out for traffic, hold hands, and stick together.
- Guidance by the complexity, diversity, and inclusion of Nature is a benefit.
  - o An expectation of new in the exploration of known.
  - o An exploration of patterns based on details of connections.
  - o Pan-disciplinary.
  - o Characterized by experience rather than theory.

- Wash your hands before you eat.

- When you go out into the world, watch out for traffic, hold hands, and stick together.

- Be aware of wonder. Remember the little seed in the Styrofoam cup: The roots go down and the plant goes up and nobody really knows how or why, but we are all like that.

- Goldfish and hamster and white mice and even the little seed in the Styrofoam cup - they all die. So do we.

- And then remember the Dick-and-Jane books and the first word you learned - the biggest word of all - LOOK."

- Periodic silence and stillness tie everything together.

  - Take a nap every afternoon.

  - Warm cookies and cold milk are good for you.

A school system based on this sort of program is going to produce academically powerful students with an abundance of self-confidence tempered by self-knowledge, empathy, compassion, humility, and curiosity about the World. As wonderful as that would be, that cannot be precisely our goal. Our goal is to do that and more than that. We must create Resilience.

> There are so many contemporary mantras reflected here, including but not limited to: mindfulness, collaboration, differentiation, inquiry-based learning, social education, constructivism, engagement, critical thinking, and self-care. The Institute for Humane Education's approach to educating "Solutionaries" explores much of the same territory.[16]

Would this system support and encourage the development of Resilience?

The answer is "Yes" because the connections between Thrivancy Education and the Resilience system are strong and can be summarized as follows:

- Economics is about social capital earned through actions that can be banked as reputation or as a sense of identity and self-knowledge that can be fully developed by,

- Self-discovery, including self-confidence and self-knowledge both inside and outside of the classroom.

- Recognition of the importance of the observer as part of the observed.

- Both success and failure, in the presence of compassion and trust, can teach.

- The standard to beat is your past performance.

- That learning is both private and corporate.
- Periodic silence and stillness tie everything together.

The ecological facet includes networks of cultural components, social norms, information resources, and perspectives such as,

- And then remember the Dick-and-Jane books and the first word you learned - the biggest word of all - LOOK."
- Live a balanced life - learn some and drink some and draw some and paint some and sing and dance and play and work every day some.
- Take a nap every afternoon.
- Warm cookies and cold milk are good for you.
- Wash your hands before you eat.

Equity has the very specific meaning that no intervention will have externalized costs. An act of resiliency must either achieve or work towards equity to be sustainable, and successful.

- Share everything.
- Play fair.
- Put things back where you found them.
- CLEAN UP YOUR OWN MESS.
- Say you're SORRY when you HURT somebody.
- Cooperation and compassion are moral imperatives rather than a cost.

Diversity, or having multiple types of all the components in the system, including, but not limited to, multiple sources of social capital, a broad array of information sources, and a variety of social, intellectual, and physical skill sets;

- expectation of new in the exploration of known.
- by the complexity, diversity, and inclusion of Nature is a benefit.
- Opportunistic in the paths taken to understanding.
- Pan-disciplinary.
- Characterized by experience rather than theory.

Meaning is a shared code including a set of rules, definitions, assumptions, concepts, values, practices, and connections that allow one to assign meaning to their reality.

- documented, available to others.

- When you go out into the world, watch out for traffic, hold hands, and stick together.

- Be aware of wonder. Remember the little seed in the Styrofoam cup: The roots go down and the plant goes up and nobody really knows how or why, but we are all like that.

- Goldfish and hamster and white mice and even the little seed in the Styrofoam cup - they all die. So do we.

- Having time to look, having time to see, and having time to reflect.

There is room for robust debate about where and how each of the elements fit together.

Independent of the details, this sort of educational system precludes the development of "tunnel vision" students and would enhance the development of Resilience.

These students would have increased opportunities to gain privately and publicly banked social capital in multiple contexts. They will have been exposed to, and learned from, diverse ecological contexts and multiple paradigms. They probably have not solved the issues of equity, but they understand that it is an issue to be addressed. In pure and simple terms, this is Thrivancy Education.

This system is not the dead-teacher, text-centric system. This system does not focus on the accepted rear-view mirror approach of the test-centric system. The focus on self-discovery inside and outside of the classroom guided by the complexity of Nature, strongly implies a rebuilding of connections with the village and the demise or at least the weakening of the marshmallow school context.

In addition, this approach demands local development. Place-based education is strengthened and reaffirmed as a legitimate goal. Biology in Texas is no longer precisely the same as Biology in upstate New York. History in Texas will be different than History in Ohio. Indeed, History and Biology might vary from one end of a state to another or even across town.

This sort of system is just very different from what is happening in most school systems in this country. We are seeing the results of over a half-century of truncated, disconnected, and increasingly narrowed schooling.

It is hard to keep up with the headlines vis-a-vis the anti-vaxxers, the anti CRT demonstrations, the book-banners, and most recently, the demand to remove mental health professionals from schools. Significant portions of the citizenry are undergoing a failure of Resilience. Some of these failures are caused by COVID shock, some by fear, and some by the swamping of reality by economically driven lies. The underlying pattern is a lack of alternative paradigms as the dominant white male cultural paradigm devolves into ideology.

> In May 2023, the Texas Legislature voted to allow school districts to replace licensed, certified, school counselors with uncertified, untrained, and unlicensed chaplains.[9]

Can we change the present system? We must if the American Idea is to survive. It will require an enormous amount of effort, patience, trust, and money. The roadblocks are huge. Consider that the present Congress, especially the Senate, is perhaps the purest archetype of the dominant, privileged, white male ideology while the House Freedom Caucus holds the country hostage. Perhaps this sort of change is a bridge too far.

Much of the governance across the country is cut from the same cloth. However, there are areas, regions, states, towns, school systems, schools, or classrooms where there is room for change. Change does not require a national wave or movement. The question becomes, can you change your backyard? Can we make a difference here and now?

Kathleen Dean Moore wrote,
Each of us has the power to make our life into a work of art that expresses our deepest values. Don't ask, *Will my acts save the world?* Maybe they won't. But ask, *Are my actions consistent with what I most deeply believe is right and good?*...
And here is the paradox of hope: that as we move beyond empty optimism and choose to live the lives we believe in, hope becomes transformed into something else entirely. It becomes stubborn, defiant courage. It becomes principled clarity. And when courageous-hearted, clear-minded people find one another, it becomes a powerful creative force for social change.[10]

Strauss and Howe's prediction that America would be entering a crisis right about now is based on their analysis of generational roles and behaviors.[11] That the crisis did not start in 2022 is, in part, the result of the behavior of the Millennial and Gen Z generations. If we are to delay the crisis indefinitely by increasing cultural Resilience, we need to change the ways we recruit the younger Gen Z and the following generations into the warp and woof of American culture.

We desperately need a "Thrivancy Education" system to increase the level of cultural resiliency, protecting the American idea as more and more of the general population begins to thrive.

The quickest way to get started is to rebuild the schools and schooling to support the development of resiliency by increasing the number of alternative paradigms available for students to pick and choose. A wealth of alternative paradigms will generate greater control, resiliency, and thrivancy.

As we begin to explore what Thrivancy Education might look like, we can stipulate that implementation will require significant changes in the present K-12 education system, but not necessarily in the ways that might be expected. Buildings probably would not have to change much. Age groupings would not have to change much. Instructional hours might change but not hugely. Support staffing requirements would not be changed significantly and therefore, supporting ancillary budgeting would not change. However, there would be a clear need for more, and more expensive, teachers to make Thrivancy Education possible.

For the 6th-8 grades, the road map has already been drawn by the EL program for reopening schools after COVID-19 closings[12] combined with Fulghum's kindergarten guide. The EL approach has been heavily and deeply tested. The addition of Fulghum's guide and the Natural History approach to kindergarten reinforces and supports the development of social intelligence and Resilience. A switch to that model would not require massive change and could be accomplished at the classroom, the school, or the system level with relative ease.

Relative ease does not mean easy. Teachers have been overwhelmed with the newest, the best, reforms ever, just to see them melt away in a year or two. Educational reform at this point must overcome an accretion of distrust and doubt. It would take time, but the success of the EL organization indicates that it can be done.

At the secondary level, the changes would be amongst the teaching faculty, including but not limited to:

- The definition of teaching faculty must include every person earning a salary on campus. That includes the classroom faculty, the kitchen crews, maintenance staff, transporters, security staff, and all the others.

Each of them represents and models different paradigms worthy of exploration.

- Classroom faculty must be trained in a primary discipline and at least one, more probably two, additional disciplines to the extent they can move across and fluently translate the shared codes, including rules, definitions, assumptions, concepts, values, practices, and connections that represent multiple disciplinary paradigms.

- The scaffolding for each student's education would be developed with the involvement of the student, a faculty advisor, mentor, coach, or guide selected jointly by the student and an experienced, almost emeritus, member of the faculty unavailable for the role.

- The number of preparations and the total number of students taught by each teacher would have to be reduced because the details of each advisee's program would necessarily need development, coordination, and daily management and would be unique.

- These mentors must model Resilience. What worked yesterday might not work today. The mentor, the student, and the village have likely changed. The role of the mentor will be to assist the student in the maintenance of their identity and self in the face of challenge, success, failure, and growth. It goes without saying, but it will be said that the mentor must scrupulously maintain their identity and function as a mentor. To do otherwise would be toxic and possibly criminal.

- In 2021, the national ratio of students to public school teacher was about 16 to 1. That is not the same as class size, but it is a reasonable proxy measure. For Thrivancy Education, that ratio must drop significantly, perhaps to 12/1. That does not mean that the traditionally focused classes are limited to 12. It does mean that the mentoring role is limited to about 12/1. Mentoring has to be focused on enhancing the complex adaptive system that produces Resilience for each student. Dealing with complicated complexity is very expensive in terms of time. This is not the same sort of thing as prepping a standard Science, History, English, or Math class. Perhaps the closest example of this sort of role is that of the Oxford Tutor.

- With appropriate training, sufficient oversight, and economic support, community members from a broad range of positions and activities must be recruited as part-time mentors and visiting faculty.

- A student schedule would include traditional classes and a yearlong Thrivancy Education program tailored to student interests and abilities as defined by the student. The Thrivancy program would have time scheduled for students to be off campus.

- Assessment would be based on a pan-disciplinary portfolio assessed by appropriate faculty, community members, and to the extent possible one or more professional practitioners.

These changes would be a tremendous start but there is one more change that needs further explanation. Independent of the educational system, absolutely nothing is more important, nor more effective, for student success than the connection between the teacher and the student.

Every teacher has three tasks. The first is to convey a body of technical, factual, or paradigmatic information. This is the subject matter of the class and probably reflected in the title, French 1, or AP Biology. This function is the easiest to deal with. It is what you learned, or not, in college. This is the "dead teacher" function that was mentioned earlier in the discussion on text-centric reforms. This is not the function that creates a memorable class.

The two remaining functions do have the potential to create a memorable class. The first is that the teacher helps the student develop a new-to-the-student paradigm. This process requires compassion on the part of the teacher where compassion is defined as the ability to meet the student where they are. Compassion means the teacher uses analogies, metaphors, and stories that can be understood and have meaning derived from and using the students' present-day paradigms. If kindergarten teachers have been successful, then teachers can build on and expand multiple extant paradigms.

Paradigm development is a slow process, and it is probably the task that experienced master teachers spend the most time and effort on. The foundation for the process is a level of social capital manifested as a level of trust. Trust by the student in the teacher, trust by the teacher in the student, and by both in the connection. Absent sufficient trust, students will resist the teacher's efforts, as well as they should. A change in the student's paradigm may mean a change in the student's identity. Given time to develop sufficient trust, the compassionate teacher can help a student to radically alter, extend, or create whole new paradigms and whole new selves.

One reason paradigm development is a slow process is the time constraints inherent in most school days. If the teacher sees a student for a one-hour class once a day, five days a week, they will be in contact with roughly three percent of the total available time, and that includes class starting and ending. If the process is going to work at all, and that is not guaranteed, more time would speed it up.

Witness military bootcamps such as those of the US Marine Corps that operates essentially 24/7. They quickly shred large parts of the recruit's paradigms and rebuild and replace them with a unique USMC paradigm that, for many, lasts a lifetime. It may have taken longer, but an equivalent sort of effect might be found with some Vietnam Veterans who were in extended combat. It may be that the element common to both situations is the shock of a shared, inescapable, irrevocable, psychological, and physical challenge.

Boot camps and combat do not fit in schools. But it is equally true that experiential education based on shared, inescapable, irrevocable, and physical challenge can be tailored to almost any school once trust has been established. The potential net result may be radical alterations, extensions, and creations of new paradigms. It doesn't always happen, but it can.

> A high school sophomore swarms up a sixty-foot challenge tower belayed by teacher. The way down is to step off the top and be lowered on belay. She is lowered. She belays the teacher up the tower. Teacher gets ready to be lowered. She panics and yells, No! The teacher says yes and steps into space. By the time they reach the ground, she is in tears and says that is the first time anybody trusted her. She changes from a hellion to graduating with honors.

The third classroom function of a teacher is to create opportunities for students to gain social capital. Teachers are very limited in their ability to directly contribute to the student's social capital. They are limited because, in a sense, the teacher's granting of social capital is, for the most part, *pro forma*. The teacher grades the papers, figures the test averages, develops a grade, writes a brief comment, and the student gains or loses some social capital.

At the edges of that process, the teacher does have some freedom with in-class behavior, commentary, face-to-face discussions to grant or build the kinds of social capital that go into the creation of self-knowledge and self-confidence.

To a great extent, the teacher can create the structure and function of the class such that students can earn peer-generated social capital. In this way, the teacher can support and modify the student's creation of self.

The accrual of social capital requires action. Moreover, it requires action in the face of risk, uncertainty, or difference. One does not earn social capital sitting at the end of a sofa watching a TV program. The student must take action, and it must be, to some degree, a public action with at least some potential costs. The action may be physical. It may be social. It may be a paradigm shift or a mix of all three.

Imagine a Calculus / Physics Advanced Placement superstar student arrives at school one morning, early in their senior year, and announces that, "If it can be reduced to an equation, it is trivial." Even if this does not indicate an explicit denial of a paradigm, it would absolutely indicate a change in focus from one paradigm to another.

A change in focus would imply a change in assumptions, values, perceptions, and understanding of the World. Because the conscious acceptance of a particular paradigm is part of one's identity, in substantial ways, this could be a whole new person. A friend could legitimately ask, "Who are you and what have you done with my friend?" The short version of the question is, "What's wrong with you?"

Imagine the costs to the student making this change in terms of settled identity, reputation, loss of connections, and loss of accrued social capital. Almost certainly, there will be a period of questioning, doubt, and disbelief on the part of his peers and faculty, during which time he is not earning much, if any, capital and is expending capital in terms of loss of identity and trust.

The teacher's role in Thrivancy Education is to create a classroom where even an AP Calculus / Physics superstar is operating with multiple paradigms on a consistent basis. Where no student becomes locked into a single paradigmatic identity. Where the Calculus / Physics student is writing poetry and performing artworks. Where paradigm switching becomes the norm.

> Is the elegance we search for in ecological explanation the same sort of elegance we search for in poetry? How is the beauty of a Mandelbrot fractal the same as, or different from, the beauty of the Mona Lisa?

Does this mean the English teacher needs to teach Calculus, or the Chemistry teacher needs to speak in Iambic Pentameter? No. It means the English teacher needs to demand steady improvement in the language from the Physics superstar and the Chemistry teacher must demand a coherent clarity from the poet when describing the Miller-Urey experiment. Every teacher must explicitly and consistently push against and explore the common boundaries of their disciplines to broaden and connect their students' paradigms.

The net result of this pattern would be a broadening of the opportunities for student performance and action. Metaphorically, instead of having enclosed, isolated rooms for English, Art, History, Science, Math, and second languages, etc., the student's education would take place in one big room with a lot of floor space and clear view from anywhere to anywhere. If the Natural History Approach is to go out into the backyard and look around, this is the functional equivalent in the school's broad intellectual, pan-disciplinary worldview.

> Disciplinary integration is not a brand-new idea. George Lucas has been advocating for it forever[13] and Schools Without Walls have functioned on multiple campuses. Thrivancy Education builds on these models with an explicit search for new student paradigms.

This is a very different style of schooling than we have now. Making this work would require, at the very minimum, the following:

- At the very core of this system is the connection between the student and the primary teacher or mentor. Every student must have confidence in the fact that at least one teacher knows them, understands them, and connects with them.

- While no teacher would be, should be, or could be held responsible for knowing all about all parts of the metaphorical room, they would constantly be pressured to broaden their horizons. This requires teachers to have time to talk to each other and explore commonalities and linkages.

> This connection can be dangerous, but it is at the core of effective teaching. Safeguards must be in place and explicit to prevent trouble. Maintenance of safeguards will be a function of senior faculty unavailable for the mentor role.

- The walls of this metaphorical room must be very porous. Students must be able to move into the village for education and experience. Community members must be able to move appropriately into the room to share specific skills and paradigms. This is a crucial step in maximizing the number of potentially variable paradigms available to students.

- While no student would be, should be, or could be held responsible for knowing all about all parts of the room, they would constantly be encouraged to explore beyond their comfort zones. To repeat, every student must have a faculty member they trust to help them navigate unfamiliar near and far spaces.

- There can be no expectation that there is a single, or best, or most valuable path around, or through, or across the room. There must be an explicit recognition that the path chosen by the student is, in fact, a significant portion of the student's identity.

- There can be no high stakes testing at the end of school. However, there must be a record and portfolio of student work with commentary from faculty, and community members, qua mentors and coaches.

Today, most systems are operating with teacher shortages. The number of students entering teacher training programs are way down, in some states over 80%, nationally down about a third. Students are not rushing to low salaries, low esteem, and little or no respect coupled with increasingly onerous, and sometimes dangerous, responsibilities.

If this country is going to be resilient and survive, the Nation, the states, cities, and towns are going to have to recognize the role master teachers play in maintaining and improving the commonwealth. If it seems that what is being suggested here is a reversion to the teacher-centric model of education that we had before Sputnik, that is true to some extent. However, this is really a student-centric system. Neither a teacher-centric model of the old style nor the industrial model will increase cultural Resilience, or protect and enhance the American Idea.

After the Civil War, men left teaching for other opportunities that were not available to women. Women became teachers and soon dominated the classrooms but not the administrative offices. These days, somewhere over 85% of teachers are women. "Even though the profession has improved over time, teaching is still widely considered "women's work," and it is also considered to be underpaid and belittled."[14]

The teacher capable of making Thrivancy Education successful is a professional educator, highly trained in at least two disciplines, creative, risk-taking, independent, compassionate, a model of Resilience, and willing to wear multiple hats, some that can put them in harm's way. The present salary scales aren't going to hack it. Not when a newly minted programmer starts in Seattle for a higher salary than a master teacher with a national certificate, a Ph.D., and 40 years' experience earns.

That cannot stand. It cannot stand for so many reasons but the first ones that leap to mind are,

- What is "women's work"? Being a five Star chef? Being a combat fighter pilot? A construction foreman? A fireman? A Fortune 500 CEO? An

Astronaut? Really? Can we still talk in those terms? Even housewives have been replaced to some degree by househusbands.

- Surely, we have each had a teacher, who in passing was a woman, who launched us into our future with skill, compassion, trust, and patience. But let's not forget about the Marine Corp Drill Sargent. Both are effective and wildly different but that difference isn't about gender.

- Students of all types, orientations, backgrounds, and skills do much better in school when the teacher demographics include a diversity of gender, races, ethnicities, socioeconomic backgrounds, spiritual beliefs, and, in short, a broad variety of cultural paradigms.

- Many of those who belittle the teaching profession have not seen a teacher, talked to a teacher, nor been in a functioning classroom since they were about 17 or 18 years old. At that age, they would not, indeed could not, see or understand the hours, the effort, nor the risks involved in walking into a class of thirty students every school day.

- As for pay, the idea that teachers work only when they are in front of a class is about the equivalent of saying a Fortune 500 CEO works only when in a meeting with all the vice presidents at once. Private conferences, public meetings, PR, and community outreach do not count, nor do annual stockholder meetings. Just as all the other training functions and teacher meetings are not counted.

Teacher salaries must change. A programmer with less than a year's experience earns a starting salary between \$75,042 and \$96,453[19]. No starting teacher earns that. The disparities between teachers and programmers get steadily wider as time goes on. How many programmers deal with a variety of inputs, the complexities, ambiguities, and lack of do-overs that teachers face every morning? Certainly some, but not many. It is time for the Nation to recognize that our future is in the hands of teachers. They need to be recognized and compensated appropriately.

> As an interesting thought experiment, what would happen if we had no teachers and no public schools. You could ask the same of any job or role, but would any other loss dissolve the Union from sea to shining sea as quickly as the loss of teachers?

Once we have the teachers in place, they would provide the foundation for building the rest of a Thrivancy Education classroom that might, at first glance, appear like the standard classroom of today. It should probably be different in at least the following ways,

- Broader range of design where we educate the hands as well as the brains,
- Even more tech heavy,
- The teacher's desk is smaller and at the rear of the classroom.
- Fewer professional wall hangings replaced by more student projects,
- Magazine racks with multiple international perspectives and languages,
- Multiple screens with a variety of local, national, international feeds, including student videos.

Everything that has been written implies that Thrivancy Education is going to be different. The daily boundaries are going to be stretched. Perspectives are going to be added. Scheduling will be flexible, and the four environmental services will be enhanced and developed. There will be a broader range of people interacting, leading, coaching, mentoring, and evaluating the student's education and performance.

The reason to make all this effort to establish Thrivancy Education is to aggressively demonstrate the existence of alternative spiritual, cultural, social, and physical paradigms. There are thousands of them. The goal of Thrivancy Education is absolutely not to recruit every child to a specific paradigm. That would just recreate the present situation with a new replacement ideology.

Of the many shibboleths associated with educational reform, the most common is "critical thinking." Are there any reforms not focused on increasing critical thinking as an important outcome? A definition of critical thinking might include: "In its exemplary form, it is based on universal intellectual values that transcend subject matter divisions: clarity, accuracy, precision, consistency, relevance, sound evidence, good reasons, depth, breadth, and fairness."[15]

Critical thinking is clearly an important objective. Every effort must be made to enhance a student's ability to achieve these skills. But it is not enough. The very best, critically thinking student might remain encapsulated, or captured, by a single paradigm. Such a trapped student may be able to think critically all day long and demonstrate very limited Resilience.

The public sphere contains many examples of critical thinkers trapped in limited paradigms, or ideologies, who cannot adapt to change. Two powerful examples are those people focused on the wording of the first half of the 2nd amendment to the exclusion of any other input, and second, the anti-vaxxers. Some are excellent critical thinkers about approaches, strategies, and effectiveness. But they cannot hear, cannot consider, and cannot accept an argument about flintlocks versus modern weapons of war or the differences between traditional and modern vaccines.

The Thrivancy Education goal of increased Resilience demands comparative or parallel thinking. The whole point of Thrivancy Education is to give the student exposure to, and experience with, a broad range of paradigms and performances to earn social capital in all its forms from diverse sources in multiple contexts and situations. Yes, it is complicated and complex, but it is precisely the over-simplification of the text-centric, test-centric and marshmallow schools that have decimated personal Resilience.

There is no one-size-fits-all recipe here for Thrivancy Education. That is precisely the point. A single recipe would be antithetical to the development of Resilience. No part of Texas can be precisely like New York. Prospect, Oregon, cannot be Trappe, Maryland. Thrivancy Education must be homegrown and vary from district to district, and maybe from school to school, or year to year. Thrivancy Education demands a tremendous degree of local control.

American education and schooling have a long tradition of local control with both good and really terrible outcomes. For almost 70 years, local control has been chipped away starting with *Brown Vs The Board of Education* in 1954. That decision, coupled with Sputnik in the same decade, triggered an increasing flow of federal funds and regulations including The War on Poverty of the 1960s.

However, it was not just the Federal and state governments reducing local control. The economics of developing and publishing curricular materials, including texts, tests, and lab kits, tended to erode local control. For many school systems, the use by colleges and universities of standardized test scores as gate keepers for post-secondary opportunities decimated local control over large parts of the curriculum. Today, local control may be the mantra, but actors outside of the system probably exert greater control over the operation of the school than the board.

Local control has sometimes produced terrible outcomes in the past. What is the process that prevents that from happening again? Perhaps there are no guarantees. Arizona is racing towards the eradication or minimizing of public education and replacing it with unregulated schools and schooling. The headlines from Florida illustrate the previous points about the damage that can be done with entrapped critical thinking. However, metaphorical fresh air, sunlight, and public viewing a powerful vaccinations preventing the most egregious cases.

Chapter 7

# Thrivancy Education Management

Schools and schooling are generally, if not the largest, certainly a major budget item for every town, county, and state in the country. Education and schooling are expensive, and Thrivancy Education is not any less expensive. In fact, it is likely to be more expensive, more complicated, and more complex. The question becomes how do you manage such a system to make sure it is doing what it says it is doing and doing so as effectively and as equitably as possible?

The standard management model is not designed to accommodate the diversity of inputs, the flexibility of the process, nor the variety of outputs that makes Thrivancy Education unique. A management model based on the natural history approach is likely to be more successful.

Every three years, the Program for International Student Assessment of the OECD gives a test to an international sample of 15-year-olds. A recent set of tests with results was administered in 2018. There are all kinds of statistics that can be found about how students and countries did on the tests, but the ones people focus on are the national averages.

Predictably, the U.S. educational system did not score particularly well. Compared to the OECD nations, in literacy, we were lower than 8. On the science test, we were lower than 6. On the Math test, we were lower than 24[1]. These rankings haven't changed appreciably over the last several educational reforms.

> It is easy to get lost in OECD numbers. This set of truncated statistics simply indicates we really cannot boast about where we have ended up.

Those are not numbers that make people shout with joy. How do we get these results? What are the reasons we don't get higher scores? Most recently, The New York Times has said, "Education experts argue vociferously about a range of potential causes, including school segregation, limited school choice, funding inequities, family poverty, too much focus on test prep and a dearth of instruction in basic skills like phonics."[2]

Slate magazine has written that these "results aren't just about K–12 test scores and curricula—they are also about academic ability tracking, income inequality, health care, child-care, and how schools are organized as workplaces for adults," and more specifically, "The OECD found that school systems with greater teacher leadership opportunities, like Canada's, outperform those like ours, in which administrators and policymakers exert more top-down control over the classroom, through scripted lessons or teacher evaluation systems that heavily weigh student test scores."[3]

Perhaps the best analysis of earlier but similar results comes from the Economic Policy Institute which finishes with a penultimate paragraph of,

> Today, threats to the nation's future prosperity come much less from flaws in our education system than from insufficiently stimulative fiscal policies which tolerate excessive unemployment, wasting much of the education our young people have acquired; an outdated infrastructure: regulatory and tax policies that reward speculation more than productivity; an over-extended military; declining public investment in research and innovation; a wasteful and inefficient health care system; and the fact that typical workers and their families, no matter how well educated, do not share in the fruits of productivity growth as they once did. The best education system we can imagine can't succeed if we ignore these other problems.[4]

Each of these critiques has merit. They represent a valid, real set of constraints and contexts that stress and constrain schools and schooling. If every issue raised here were addressed, schools would do better, much better, no doubt. But each of these statements has a perspective from above and beyond the classroom, but not from within the classroom.

This is an example of not using the Resiliency Paradigm. There is no use of the Natural History nor the Systems theory approaches. The Natural History approach to understanding American schools and schooling would have gone to where it happens. The success or failure of schools on these tests is not about school systems, or even schools. Success or failure occurs in the classroom. Even more specifically, it occurs in the connections between student and teacher. None of the critics or analysts went into the place where it all happens to see what happens.

The Natural History approach would have said, "Let's go look in the backyard," only this time it would have been "Let's go look in the classroom."

The Natural History approach would have been,

- An expectation of new in the exploration of known.

All classrooms are the same, but each classroom is precisely different from every other classroom. The discovery of the difference is the discovery of the new.

- An exploration of patterns based on details of connections.

It is always about the connections: teacher-confidence, student-teacher, student-student, student-space, student- baggage, student-confidence, teacher- administration, student-others outside, etc.

- Pan-disciplinary.

The metaphor here tells the class story as completely and truthfully as possible about the socio-economic, cultural, and psychological aspects.

- Recognition of the importance of observer as part of the observed.

As the observer comes through the door, the classroom system changes. A new sub-system has just been added to an already functioning system. Connections are formed instantly, perhaps as alliances to exclude, or perhaps to include but disarm, or perhaps just to include. Change has already occurred.

- Characterized by experience rather than theory.

Is there really a single idea or theory about the good, bad, or ugly classroom? Every classroom is the same. Every single classroom has unique inputs that change daily if not minute to minute. Therefore, every classroom is unique. The experience here is to identify the patterns and connections that constitute the system.

- Opportunistic in the paths taken to understanding.

There can be no specific recipe, process, or protocol for what happens during a visit to a classroom. There are patterns, connections, and understandings that can be determined and established before an observation, but underway, the observation must take advantage of the moment.

- And documented, available to others.

The documentation of the observations is an area in need of development. Certainly, the story of the classroom can be told but how to make that story part of an analytical or comparative database is a stark and difficult issue. Really excellent classrooms come in so many different forms. It seems to be similar to "True Love," difficult or impossible to define but easier to recognize. However, a solid foundation has been set with the application of General Systems Theory. All classes are systems. Therefore, all classes can be held up to that rubric.

What has been described flies in the face of the normal analytical, or management, approach where the perspective is from the outside, using dimensions or criteria, focused on input/output ratios, efficiencies, and appearances. A classroom evaluator faced with this approach might throw up their hands and say there are no protocols, standards or norms. It is way too "go with the flow" to produce useful results.

There are two responses to this reaction. First, there are absolute norms. The unsuccessful classroom is going to break norms that almost everybody would recognize: norms about racism, sexism, rankism, bullying in any form, veracity, safety, and effectiveness. Classrooms that break, or even approach, these norms must be called out, broken apart, and rebuilt, often with a new teacher.

A second response addresses the issue of comfort or discomfort evaluators, administrators, managers, and teachers might have with the complexity of the natural history approach to uncertainty, nonlinearity, and emergence. Ashby's Law, the First Law of Cybernetics, says that the more complex the system, the more complex the management must be. One can analyze, evaluate, and manage only what one knows. If a system is more complex than management knows, then the system is doing, or failing to do, all sorts of things that management knows nothing about.

> Ashby's law is also known as The Law of Requisite Variety and states variety, and only variety, can absorb variety.[5]

Two examples will illustrate the point. Back in the day when women were rarely in charge, if you needed assistance in finding out about or navigating through, an organization, the first question was, "Do you want to talk to the man in charge or the woman who knows what's going on?" The executive could and would talk about the mission, direction, and identity of the organization, but the woman, often an "Assistant," knew who was doing what, whom to talk to, where the process was, and how to get things done.

A second example is, "Working to the rule" by those not allowed to go on strike. Every organization has a rule or policy book, but the people doing the job have workarounds, short cuts, and exceptions that allow them to get the job done quickly, effectively, and efficiently. Working to the rule quickly brings an organization to a huge slow-down or to a halt.

The concern generated by Ashby's Law about the required complexity of any evaluation can be addressed if the Systems Theory Paradigm is applied, starting with an Evaluability Assessment (EA). Metaphorically, the Lewis and Clark expedition was an EA of the Pacific Northwest. Before the expedition, there was a great deal of information, opinion, perspective, and experience already known about the area. But there was no framework of agreement about how all of it fit together. Lewis and Clark started to create that framework.

An EA is an exploration of whether or not a program, process or organization can be effectively evaluated or managed.[6] An EA establishes a framework for undertaking and understanding an evaluation. If such a common framework cannot be established amongst those using the product, an evaluation will be an expensive waste of time and management of the system will be problematic at best.

An EA involves a wide array of stakeholders, and reviews the documentation of program development or management to get agreement, or explicit disagreement, about the following sorts of statements:

- The mission, goals, and objectives are clear, realistic, and commonly understood by everybody involved including boards, administrators, teachers, students, parents, and the village.

- The theory and logic of the change to be achieved are explicit and rational.

- The types and levels of the required inputs and outputs are sufficient to achieve programmatic goals.

> Many school board meetings dissolve into shouting matches, threats, and Chaos because the players have unexamined, unexpressed opinions, perspectives, and understandings of basic elements of schooling. No program evaluation is useful here and effective management is almost impossible.

- The map of the process, including intermediate steps and the required personnel, is explicit.

- The meanings ascribed to various levels of indicators of the inputs, outputs, and process are agreed to.

- The performance indicators are available or can be made available.

For almost any program, but especially for a complicated and complex program such as Thrivancy Education, an EA is a time-consuming effort and will require the investment of money and people. Evaluability Assessments have rarely been done for schools or schooling. The fact that we do not have explicit agreements or explicit, detailed disagreements is why Chaos so often swirls around schools in this country. Evaluations and management under these circumstances will be, at best, difficult and, at worst, impossible.

The situation is not going to get better soon. Across a state, or county, or town, there may be little agreement about the varieties of costs, or the process, or what the outcomes should be for schools and schooling. Multiple states have pending legislation to allow parents to stop a history course on a whim or because their child is embarrassed by the subject. As pointed out earlier, some locales have passed laws that make the teaching of a history that somebody does not like subject to multimillion dollar fines. Florida is threatening to block the A.P. Psychology course over a segment on gender and sexual identity and has blocked the A.P. Black History course on whatever "wokeness" is about.

Or we have a legislative hearing, where a question is asked of a rural superintendent, "What use would someone on the McDonald's career track have for Algebra 1?" before concluding, "There's a need for retail workers, for people who know how to flip a pizza crust."[7]

These days, if an EA is not done, there is a very good possibility that any analysis, evaluation, or management will be dealing with disagreements, often vehement, about the structure, the process, and goals of the program. If there is ambiguity in the description of the program, or the meaning and significance of the metrics used, an evaluation is worse than useless. It squanders confidence in the process, burns time and resources, and generates ill-will and low morale.

An Evaluability Assessment is not a magic process that ends these disagreements. What an EA starts to do is make explicit the beliefs, assumptions, and mental models that school boards, teachers, parents, students, and the Village have about schools and schooling. An EA is an opportunity for the school to make community ideas about what the school is, what it should do, and how to measure it all, explicit as a framework for building school-community connections and networks.

> An EA may provide a solid foundation for Russell L. Ackoff's "Idealized Design" process.[10]

In short, an EA can start rebuilding the village support that may have atrophied over time by loss of local control, lack of communication, and misinformation. It may sound cynical, but an EA is a huge opportunity to build local support by increasing local understanding of the often unseen and unexpected complexity that is a school.

An EA starts with an examination of foundational documents including:

- National and State constitutions and regulations,
- Board Meeting Minutes,

- System Budgets for at least ten years,

- Any accreditation documents,

- Superintendent, principal, faculty meeting minutes,

- Aggregated system statistics about personnel, student outcomes, etc.

- Locally important documents.

There are two initial hurdles to getting this done. The first is who, and how many, should do it? Who can support the kind of time and effort commitment? Who has the experience and skill set? Who has the community's trust? How much will they be paid and who is doing the selection? These are the first questions to be asked, and

> The people doing the EA and the people interviewed later in the process probably should be selected via an explicit, stratified random sampling process.

they are not easy. Without putting too much weight on it, this is the classic: who watches the Watchmen?

There is no automatic correct answer, but there are many automatically wrong answers. People with overt political agendas, conflicts of interest, and all the rest of the obvious markers should not be selected. It is entirely possible these days that there is no way the selection process will keep everybody on board. However, if the process is botched, the result will be a waste of resources and goodwill.

The second hurdle is what to look for. The question might be a fundamental query "What do we really want from our Schools?" or "Are we doing the right things in the right way?" An evaluation may be targeted on questions about the sufficiency of inputs, processes, or outcomes, or the questions can be focused on efficiency, and value for the dollar.

Whatever the questions are will determine the scope of work. Broad questions of socioeconomic efficacy and equity may require a great deal of digging and research. A narrow question about a program supporting the health

> The question can be asked. What do we want ideally from our schools? The school community can explore answers in a manner similar to the Ideal Design Process.

and welfare of students may require less. In either case, when looking at the foundational documents, it is important to recognize a change that makes a difference: a policy change, a budgetary change, facility alterations, personnel changes, program changes, or, in some cases, a change in context and environmental input.

Schools and schooling are complex systems. Any change in one component may reverberate through the system. So, again, the Natural History Approach is needed. These initial phases are similar to the situation for Lewis and Clark. Lots of people have been here before. There is a great deal of disparate, disconnected, contradictory, and incomplete information out there. The goal here is to develop a map of the history, components, and connections that have produced the system being evaluated and then managed.

A fundamental rule is to remember the map is not the territory. Very few maps will contain the informal or non-formal connections, the workarounds, and the understandings that allow the system to work. This first map always needs further work discovering, describing, and identifying the components and connections only hinted at in the initial stages of an EA.

The process of filling in the first map is the process of talking to a wide range of stakeholders with different perspectives on the system or program. These conversations are structured by questions about the inputs, structures, processes, and outcomes that have been identified initially. The internet has multiple lists of appropriate questions that can be used as guidelines.

Some lists, for multi-faceted, large programs, are extensive and some lists are short, but they all include the following sorts of general questions:

- What is your connection with the program?

- How much do you know or care about the program in question?

- What are the appropriate goals or outcomes of the program?

> It would be wonderful if every participant answered these questions before every board or legislative meeting. We do not need agreement to start, but agreement, or explicit disagreement, at the end allows more effective management.

- Is the design of the program likely to be successful?

- What specific challenges does the program have to overcome?

- What are reasonable expectations of program performance?

- How does one know if the program is meeting these expectations?

- Has the program performance changed over time?

- Have there been unintended consequences?

- What might be changed if expectations are not met or merit improvement?

- Should the program be continued?

These interviews or discussions are not intended to be persuasive or to achieve lock-step agreement. The goal here is to make sure that everybody is talking about the same program, even if they disagree vehemently about it.

While an EA may discover and make explicit different perspectives, understandings, or expectations, the purpose of the EA is to find, and perhaps to develop, common ground. To the extent that common ground exists, a program can be evaluated and administered or managed. To the extent that common ground is absent, the issues become political and not managerial and must be resolved elsewhere.

Once an EA is done, it will need to be reviewed and renewed periodically. How often depends on the size, complexity, and dynamics of the program in question. Thrivancy Education may be large or small, but it will certainly involve many bits and pieces and the involvement of many people in a constantly changing structure. However, the second, third, and fourth EA's will get easier and easier with each one. The rationale will not change appreciably. The documentation will be a case of updating. The stakeholders are the dynamic element. The broad range of participants must be surveyed consistently, not constantly, to monitor the inherent dynamism of Thrivancy Education.

Part of the on-going monitoring of the EA is accomplished by teachers. An informal, on-the-fly EA is precisely what successful teachers are doing from the time they park their car in the morning until they leave. They read the stakeholders as they come through the classroom door, and they listen. They have a process and metrics in mind. They work to get agreement about the validity of the metrics, and they work on agreement about what the outcomes are to be. And they do the same sort of thing multiple times during the class in a manner that is implicitly Natural History. Their aggregated inputs are crucial, but not sufficient, to maintain the validity of the more formal EA process. You must keep talking to teachers and everybody else on campus. After all, everybody on campus is considered faculty.

A well done, complete EA will get rid of all sorts of ambiguity and disagreements while celebrating the uniqueness of every instance of Thrivancy Education because every component is variable: the teacher, the village, the students, and the location. With a well-done EA, management of Thrivancy Education becomes no more challenging nor dramatically different than effectively administering any K-12 program.

A well done, complete EA has the potential to lay a trap for an administration. That trap comes in the form of thinking that broad agreement in an EA would be automatic grounds for setting "standards." Obviously, there is room for system wide, school wide and program wide standards about health, safety, support, and, in general, the environmental services discussed earlier. Standards impose and compel uniformity.

If an EA demonstrates broad agreement on some element, that unanimity might be used to forge a standard. "We all agree this should be the student level of achievement, therefore, let's agree this level is success." Suddenly, we have a standard every child should achieve. And standards of this type drive a stake through the creativeness and richness of Thrivancy Education.

It is this creativeness and richness that allows Thrivancy Education to support and encourage resiliency in students. It is this resiliency that means students do not get lost or left behind. Again, Lewis and Clark provide an excellent model. Not every expedition member followed the same path, did the same things, nor had the same experiences on the way to and from Astoria, but, equally important, only one was lost, to appendicitis.

> York, Clark's rifle-carrying and voting slave, was an important part of the expedition's safe passage. His experience was unique, but he more than earned the respect and friendship of the rest of the crew and seems to have ended his days with the Crow Indians.

In many communities, the schools are the pivot point that the community identifies with and revolves around. In most communities, nothing gets a bigger portion of the taxes; nothing gets more airtime or column inches. Schools are important to the community's identity and function. A well-done EA removes much of the ambiguity about the community schools but even with the increased clarity, the question becomes how do you manage such a system to make sure it is doing what it says it is doing, and doing so as effectively and as equitably as possible?

Public schools are run by elected boards, and, until recently, there were often dedicated, long-term, board members providing continuity while budgeting large sums of money and dealing with complex personnel, programmatic, legal, and ethical issues. These are issues important to any community and board meetings might get heated, but the issues were rarely life or death and, for the most part, consensus was possible.

However, since about 2016, school boards have become more and more enmeshed in the toxic national politics of public health mandates, QAnon fantasies, and a whole range of gender identity, social, racial, and cultural issues. Given the dominant white male cultural ideology and lack of Resilience, consensus is difficult, especially because there is no longer

> Founded in 2021, Moms for Liberty, exploded onto the scene building on the frustrations of Covid-19, financed by the scavenger oligarchs to wreak havoc, banning books, and terrorizing kids. Huge money and loud virulence raised their profile in the Republican Party as a short-lived example of, "Do as I say, not as I do."

broad agreement on what schools could, should, or would do. The administration and management of schools has become contentious.

The standard management models are not designed to provide an understanding of the diversity of inputs, flexibility of process, nor the variety of outputs that makes Thrivancy Education unique. The standard model is just too incomplete and simplified to do so. While a well-done EA is a solid launching pad for the management of Thrivancy Education, the traditional approach to management based on the concepts encapsulated in the "upside-down-tree" diagram of organizational structure will not work.

There is a story, perhaps apocryphal, that the upside-down tree was first developed to assign blame for an 1850s train wreck. That story may or may not be true, but it is correct in the sense that that diagram does nothing but assign blame. Because there are two incorrect assumptions in the diagram or model, there is no possibility that it reflects how a complex organization functions.

The first incorrect assumption is that all command-and-control communication in an organization is vertical. All the direction comes from the top, and all the reports of success or failure go to the top. Does anybody work in that sort of organization? An organization where no lunchroom, water fountain, bus stop, or parking lot conversations take place?

In schools, the overwhelming volume of communication is horizontal or local. Students talk, teachers talk, parents talk, and they all talk to each other. Most of that talk does not involve principals or boards. In fact, principals and boards often have little idea about what is being talked about or being said. But it is precisely in these horizontal discussions where many, probably most, issues, good or bad, are discussed and dealt with.

The second incorrect assumption is that skills and knowledge increase as you go up the model towards the upper levels. That might have been true for many jobs decades ago. The shop foreman may have been more experienced and capable than the worker, for the majority of tech-based, skill-based, and context-sensitive, occupations that is simply no longer true. The supervisor cannot do the job as well as the worker. A school principal may be an expert on how to teach at a general, reified level, but is unlikely to step into a Math, Science, Mandarin, or English class and teach that class as well as the teacher. There is just too much that the principal does not know about the class and cannot find out as they walk through the door.

Most CEOs of large organizations can wander off to attend conferences, give speeches, or spend time "with the family" skiing in the Alps, and nobody much misses them. Why? Primarily because while they are the public face of the organization, they have few or no production skills contributing to how the organization functions. There are exceptions, but they are rare.

If we can assume that the people doing the job are the best at doing so, then the highest goal of any administrative system is to maintain coordination and control while maximizing the autonomy of those doing the job and producing an output. One of the most successful road maps to achieve this end is the Viable System Model developed by Stafford Beer.

The Viable Systems Model (VSM) requires looking at and managing, organizations in a whole new way. Over the years, a great deal has been written about how to implement and apply the paradigm, including Beer's *Diagnosing the System for Organizations*.[8] Perhaps the clearest discussion of the approach is *The Fractal Organization* by Patrick Hoverstadt.[9]

To do justice to the power and nuance of the VSM is beyond the scope of this book. However, a brief discussion will demonstrate why the VSM approach makes Thrivancy Education possible where the standard administrative approach would effectively kill the effort.

To be viable to exhibit Resilience in the face of change, an organism, or an organization, must be able to collect, process, and respond to multiple sources of information in a timely and effective fashion by allowing a degree of functional autonomy to five types of organizational subsystems, while maintaining a high degree of coordination, and cohesiveness. The five types of subsystems are: production, coordination, management, research and development, and governance.

It is important to understand that here, "subsystem" focuses more on a function rather than a structure. For a school the production subsystem is often a classroom. However, a production subsystem might equally be associated with a theater stage, an athletic field, an off-campus project, a maintenance shop, the kitchen, or the bus barn.

The subsystem boundaries are frequently diffuse and recursive. A single subsystem function might be done by multiple people at the same time and at the same or different levels of the school system. A teacher in the classroom will do all five functions simultaneously as will the principal and the superintendent.

As an observer moves through different levels of the organization from the classroom to the school, individuals may spend more, or less, time and effort on a given subsystem. A teacher keeps some record of grades as part of the daily routine, but it is part of a registrar's definition.

It is equally important to understand that, as in any system, the links and connections are as important as the functions. The VSM is only viable when the five subsystems maintain a degree of autonomy but are tightly and effectively linked by communication channels.

It is also important to recognize that the VSM is a recursive model. If the school is a system, then the classroom is a subsystem. But the class is simultaneously a system containing the same five subsystems. Thus, a class is a subsystem of a school and is identified as a production subsystem, while the teacher is a combination of the coordination, management, and R&D subsystems for the class. The model has the same structures but different contents at every level of the system, from the district to the school, the classroom, and finally to the individual student.

The five subsystems are:

Production: In VSM terminology, these are system 1s. Every system must do something. If there is nothing happening, a bunch of bits and pieces is not a system. It is just a pile. System 1s are the production units in the viable system. In schools, System 1s will be the classes, the teams, the kitchen, the counselors, the development or PR, maintenance, the clubs, PTA, etc. A large high school will easily have hundreds of System 1s.

Coordination: In VSM terminology, these are named System 2. In a VSM, System 1s have a degree of autonomy. That means that from time to time, they run into each other, or stumble around and get in each other's way. System 2 is primarily a coordination and allocation of resources function, allowing System 1 to maintain their functions and to do so without conflict. In a school, examples of System 2 functions would include setting the bell schedule, scheduling space for classes, keeping student records, scheduling substitutes, paying utility bills, doing payroll, and scheduling transportation. If System 1 needs more of a consumable supply or needs maintenance, System2 provides those supplies or maintenance provided it is within the budget. System 2 does not determine the budget, the pay scale, or the length of class blocks, nor set graduation requirements. System 2 implements and coordinates the decisions made by the administration or System 3.

System 3 is the day-to-day management of the school. The goal of System 3 is to implement the School Board's decisions and to minimize oscillation in the face of potential production or environmental turbulence. This is the function that addresses the need for substitutes, weather delays, increasing costs of bus fuel, scheduling special events, back-to-school-nights, or any of the thousand other decisions that keep the school operating in the face of change. While System 3 does not set graduation requirements, it may have the option of determining which History or Math courses will be offered to fulfill the requirements.

System 3 is focused on meeting the day-to-day needs of the operational units of the organization. Are we meeting the criteria or outputs that were set a while back. Are students in class? Are teachers being paid on time? Does the athletic team have the support that it needs to be safe? The best possible day is a day when System 3 is almost invisible. If we assume that the dawn starts a new, unblemished day, the goal of System 3 is to maintain the status quo, to absorb any vagaries and maintain the day as unblemished and smooth as possible.

System 4 is a research and development function, and as such is inherently disruptive. System 4 is Janus-faced. System 4 looks inward and asks, "Are we doing what we say we are doing, and could we do it better?" System 4 also looks outward and asks, "What is there in our environment that represents an opportunity or a threat for our continued operations?" Absent an effective System 4, an organization is unlikely to remain viable.

An effective System 4 challenges System 3 by pointing out that today's status quo may not be the best way forward or replicable tomorrow. There is always at least some tension between System 3, management, and System 4, R&D. Management's focus is on maintaining the best possible status quo. System 4's focus is on change; either doing what we do better or by addressing an external opportunity or threat. While

Any organization without a high functioning interaction between systems 3 & 4, will make errors of commission or omission. Examples of commission; the Edsel, New Coke, Heinz purple ketchup, Google +, and Cheetos Lip Balm. Examples of missed opportunities or omissions: IBM missing PC's, and, generally, the missed warnings about 9/11 and 1/6.

management's response may be positive or negative, R&D's demands for change cannot be dismissed out of hand.

If the issues raised by System 4 cannot be addressed through relatively minor administrative fiat or if System 3 and System 4 cannot come to an agreement about change versus continuity, it is time for System 5 to make a choice. System 5 is about organizational identity. At the school level, System 5 is the Board, acting through a superintendent. System 5 develops the mission statement, supporting policies, budgets, and annual goals or objectives. These developments are based on data from System 2s, and inputs from 3s and 4s.

System 5 should not have much to do. Production, coordination, R&D, and management function on a daily, even hourly basis, but the System 5 function should spend most of the time quiescent. Mission statements probably do not have to change all that often, wholesale policy changes are probably not frequently required, budgeting is an annual event and not too noisy. Goals and objectives will be set and reviewed from time to time.

At least, that was the way it was not too long ago. Most Board meetings were just not that exciting. Most boards operated on the information generated by the R&D function of the superintendent and their staff. For many boards, that has changed. Board meetings are being overwhelmed and rendered difficult by an emotional, vociferous onslaught delivered under the aegis of Moms for Liberty. Membership on the local school board has become one of the more exciting, or terrifying, opportunities in town.

> As COVID recedes, the temperature of board meetings may be dropping, especially as Moms for Liberty fall farther into disrepute to be replaced by quieter adult and student voices.

What the board should not do, ever, is to interfere directly with the operation of a production or system 1 unit, without going through the 3s and 2s. As was pointed out earlier, there is almost no chance that System 5, the Board, knows as much about the productive functions as the teachers, coaches, kitchen staff, or maintenance staff doing the work.

The board directly interfering with a System 1 is generally hugely counterproductive. Prime examples right now are what is happening in Florida Advanced Placement classes as boards and politicians micromanage the educational process. More examples can be found across the States where boards are passing judgement on specific classroom libraries, lesson plans, and decorative posters.

If one were to draw a map of the five Systems, and their links, it might look like this.

**Figure 7.1.** The Viable Systems Model

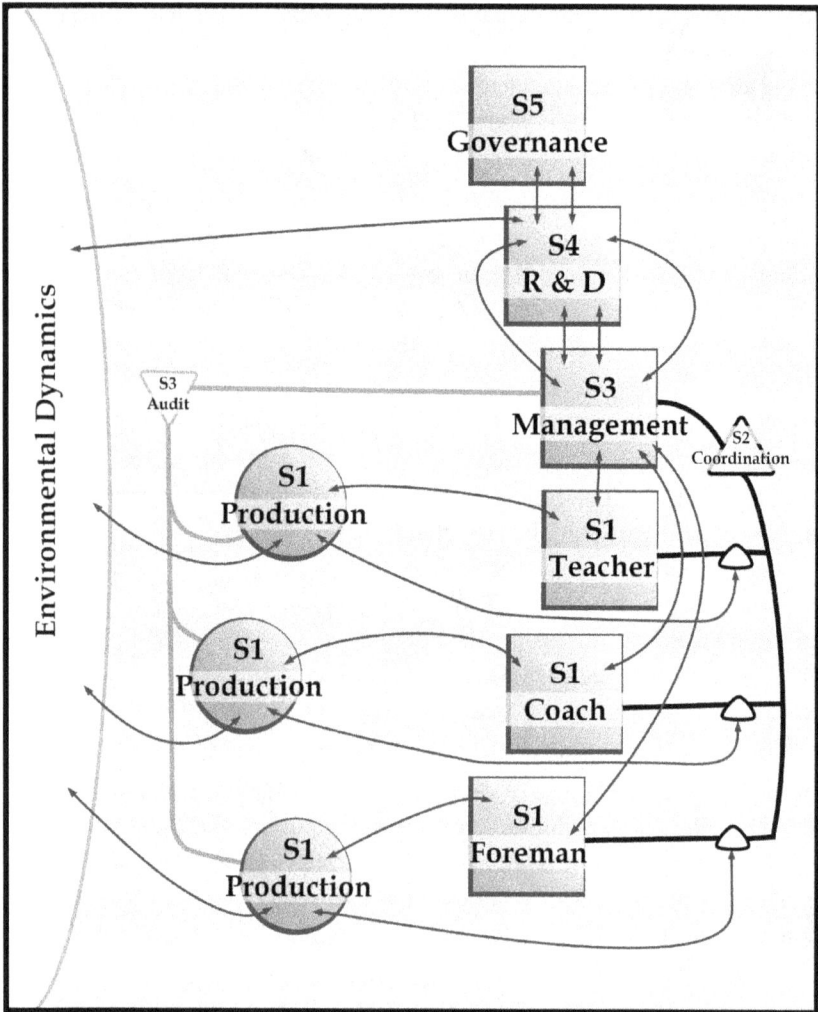

The arrows connecting the VSM subsystems represent primarily the formal, institutionalized communication channels, each of which has multiple links. The nonformal, ephemeral, channels are not mapped in this diagram, even though they are crucially important. Each of the formal channels has information flows characterized by volume and variety. High volume is generally correlated with low variety. Low volume tends to be associated with high variety.

> The creation of nonformal connections, positive or negative, within the school will be primarily the outcome of the Audit channel.

The Routine Channel that connects the Systems 1 and 2 is generally a high volume, low variety connection between all the System 1s and System 2, production to coordination. In schools, the routine channel would include class attendance reports, request for consumables, grade reports, requests for field trip transport, daily bulletins, early departure announcements, calendars, bell schedules, room assignments, scheduling back-to-school events, maintenance requests, and any one of hundreds of other communications up and down that take place on a frequent or recurring basis and are handled routinely. This is a high-volume channel, but the messages tend to be repetitive, ordinary, and to a degree low-variety, and predictable. There should not be many huge surprises in either direction, up or down, on this channel.

> The nature of Faculty and staff meetings may vary from moment to moment, time to time, and certainly by organizational culture. Depending on the moment, they could serve any or all the channels.

The Command channel is a lower volume, higher variety, direct connection between System 3 and the System 1s.

For System 1, this is the channel where a call for assistance is generated. Sometimes the call is for clarification or general guidance, but this is also the critical channel for an actual or metaphorical fire alarm about disruption, emergency, and immediate assistance. What should not be happening are reports of normalcy from System 1. Because of the nature of this channel, it allows for both formal and nonformal communications. Sometimes, it is a write-up on a form, and, sometimes, you just shout long and loud.

From the administrative view, this is the channel for response to System 1s. If a System 1 needs assistance, this is where it is communicated or provided. The flows in this channel from System 3 to the System1s tend to be low volume and high variety concerning physical, human, social, technical, and other assistance as needed.

> Effective use of this channel is all about identity, morale, and confidence for the school, the faculty, and the kids. There may be issues, but together, we can deal with them, and watch us succeed.

Although it sounds as though this channel is all about issues and problems, it can equally be about successes. This is the channel where the teacher invites the administration, or System 3 in general, to admire a student's or a class's success. This is the channel where the administration can call attention to championships, athletic or academic, or any special event, award, or kudos. In terms of school identity, pride, and culture, this is a crucial channel to use well and wisely.

The special channel is often referred to as the audit channel. However, "audit" has a negative check-up connotation that this channel should not have. A better name for this channel is "Management by Wandering Around." This channel is not an evaluation, checking up, or judgmental channel. This is an educational channel where Systems 3 and 4 can be taught and can learn about how System 1s must function in their environments. This is a channel that reassures administration that what they think is happening is happening. It must be structured to handle moderate volume and high, very high, variety.

This special channel is also where the Natural History Approach is crucial. If the administration wanders around with a checklist full of little boxes, this simply becomes another incomplete, unproductive, evaluation tool. This point is so important, it is worth repeating what was written earlier:

The Natural History approach includes,

- An expectation of new in the exploration of known. All classrooms are the same, but each classroom is precisely different from every other classroom. The discovery of the difference is the discovery of the new.

- An exploration of patterns based on details of connections. It is always about the connections: teacher-confidence, student-teacher, student-student, student-space, student-baggage, student-confidence, teacher-administration, student-others outside, and on and on.

- The pan-disciplinary approach. Here tells the subsystem's story about the socio-economic, cultural, psychological, and other aspects as completely and truthfully as possible.

- Recognition of the importance of observer as part of the observed. As the observer comes through the door, the classroom system changes. A new sub-system has just been added to the functioning system. Connections are formed almost instantly; perhaps as alliances to exclude, or perhaps to include but disarm, or perhaps just to include.

- Characterized by experience rather than theory. Is there really a single idea or theory about the good, bad, or ugly classroom? Every single classroom is the same. Every single classroom has unique inputs that change daily, if not minute to minute. Therefore, every classroom is unique. The experience here is to identify the patterns and connections that constitute the system.

- Opportunistic in the paths taken to understanding. There can be no specific recipe, process, or protocol for what happens during a visit to a classroom. There are patterns, connections, and understandings that can be determined and established before an observation, but underway the observation must take advantage of the moment.

- And documented, available to others. The documentation of the observations is an area in need of development. Certainly, the story of the classroom can be told but how to make that story part of an analytical, or comparative database is a stark and difficult issue. Really excellent classrooms come in so many different forms. It seems to be similar to "True Love," difficult or impossible to define but easier to recognize. However, a solid foundation has been set with the application of a previously completed EA. All classes are systems. Therefore, all classes can be held up to that rubric based on the EA.

At this point, somebody throws up their hands and says, "Who has time for this?" The answer is, "You must.." Besides educating the System 4s and 3s, this channel, done correctly, generates trust on the part of System 1s where trust is the product of a complex interaction of shared integrity, shared understandings, and shared acceptance of risk. Absent this channel, none of that sharing is guaranteed and, at best, is reduced.

> Board members may be political beings. If they use the audit channel, they need to hold their politics in abeyance and be trained in the Natural History paradigm. If they do otherwise, Trust may wither. As a thought experiment, imagine a school with zero subsystem-to-subsystem trust, and the kind of education provided. These may be the schools one hears about as armed camps.

The trust generated provides the single best way to have some understanding of all that non-formal communication that is constantly flowing through and around the school. The management of appropriate System 1 autonomy in the absence of trust is difficult, if not impossible, because little, if any, of the nonformal communication and information will be available to Systems 3 and 4. Absent Trust, the only option is coercion, and we are right back where we started; complexity is dead, Resilience is thwarted, and Thrivancy Education never gets off the ground.

# Chapter 8

# Can the American Idea Survive?

The short answer is "yes." What is ironic is that the system is flashing red because of internal stress and inequities, but we spend far more time, effort, and increasingly rare resources to defend ourselves from outer threats. The U.S., with less than 5% of the World's population, has approximately 37% of the World's expenditures on boats, planes, rockets, bullets, and soldiers. Roughly 25% of those expenditures goes into salaries which is a huge support for the lower and middle class. That is an infusion of over $178 billion dollars. That leaves more than $500 billion for, broadly speaking, hardware. Some of that money goes into peoples' pockets and supports the system for the designers, builders, and retirees' pension funds. But the largest per capita share goes, again, to the 1%.

The other counter-productive aspect of the hardware budget is that once a plane is built, when a ship is launched, all that is a sunk cost. The ship and the plane produce nothing. They become a sinkhole of maintenance and material that contributes little to the national commonwealth and eventually ends up parked in junkyards along the coasts or in the deserts.

Neither a heavily armed military nor a militarized police force will prevent the internal collapse and dissolution of the American idea. The weapons that threaten the American Idea are the in-your-face technologies, i.e. Facebook, TikTok, or that site formerly known as Twitter, combined with the lying for dollars business plans, manipulated by a network of local and international scavenger oligarchs. Their weapons are the dollars used to buy and sell decision makers. They are getting richer and accumulating influence and control. In 1990, the richest 1% of Americans held approximately 5% of all privately held wealth. At the start of 2021, they held 36% and were on track to hold 72% by 2030.[1] Strauss and Howe suggested that their predicted crisis might be over by 2030[2].

The crisis very well might be over by 2030. The oligarchs and the rest of the one or two percent at the top of the hierarchy, in their mirrored bubbles, do not know it yet, but the system is bankrupt and starting to collapse.

- In 2020, roughly 43% of Americans were underinsured or totally lacked any health insurance. As a nation, we spend, per capita, twice as much as the rest of the World, and we have the shortest life expectancy of any OECD country. Our short life expectancy is, in part, because we kill each other and ourselves with lies and guns.

> Billionaires aren't okay — for their mental health, it's time to drastically raise their taxes. From threatening cage matches, measuring genitalia, to backing RFK Jr., billionaires prove too much money detaches a person from reality.[3]

- For fifty years, the poverty rate in the United States has remained stable at close to 23%, with roughly 12% living in dire poverty.[4]

- After we finished the original interstate highway infrastructures, we underfunded both the physical, i.e., roads and trains, and the social, i.e., schools, hospitals, and cultural institutions, while moving $51 trillion up the hierarchy to the scavenger oligarchs.[5] We have achieved the status of being the inequality champion of the OECD.

People are starting to pay attention. In 2008, the last time the top of the hierarchy stood shoulder-to-shoulder with overlapping shields to form a defensive shield wall, individuals and locales were decimated, but for a huge portion of us, it wasn't really personal. It has become personal. It has become about controlling my identity, my body, my future, and my life, or it is all about somebody I know, like, or love. When it becomes a personal story, it suddenly becomes more important, worth talking about and acting on.

People are beginning to talk. The continuing headlines about the ethical lapses of Robert's Court are just another stream that erodes the standing of, and respect for, the Court as they sullenly refuse to develop a response. As this is written, at least two states have announced they will, for better or for worse, ignore the Court and run on state law. Several states are building contingency plans to ignore or reduce the impact of future court decisions about a broad range of issues. Texas has decided to ignore the Supreme Court on who controls the national borders. As the election of 2024 approaches, and the Court is called on to decide fundamental, constitutional issues, "The Stench of Corruption is growing Stronger Around the Supreme Court."[6]

The 2024 election season is well and truly started. Most people are not paying attention yet, but the Republican Party is clearly rocked back on its heels. In several states, at the state level, the party is bankrupt, but the legislatures are still passing laws that put both adults and children at risk. Where draconian, anti-abortion laws have already been passed, the legislatures have moved on to specifically attacking trans-youth and the full range of the LGBTQIA+ community in general. In their spare time, they support the "Moms for Liberty" banning books, taking over school systems, and doing their best to create Chaos for kids and teachers. Again, it bears repeating, almost everything the Republican Party is focused on is all about controlling my identity, my body, my future, and my life, or it is all about somebody I know, like, or love. When it becomes a personal story, it suddenly becomes more important, worth talking about and acting on.

> Much of the Chaos is created by about 10 people trying, as of today, to defund Ukraine's defense. They are affectionately becoming known as "Putin's Congressional Beachhead."

At the national level, the House has become so dysfunctional as to sink into what in most cases would be irrelevance. To date, they have taken about 724 votes, the most in over a decade, and passed 34 bills, the fewest in a century. They go home for a long breaks without doing anything about the rot threatening the American Idea at the bottom of the hierarchy. To wit:

- socioeconomic inequities based on past and extant racism, genderism, and rankism.

- system-wide bankruptcies including climate change, material shortages, ecological decay, and instability.

- social injustices including lack of food and water security, voter rights, and social mobility.

It is just so important to understand that what the Republicans are focused on is not some distant question about economics, or even guns and taxation. The party is focused on us as individuals, what we are allowed to

> ...the drop in the arrest rate over time is entirely accounted for by the current generation of young adults, who are busted 23 percent less frequently than prior generations were at their age.[7]

do with our bodies, our health, our children and, generally, with our lives. They have made politics intensely and immediately personal.

While the far right-wing has been focused on creating bad news for individuals, they have been overtaken by a veritable wave of personal good news. Inflation is down. There are more jobs than workers. Wage increases are beating inflation. The cost of eggs has dropped like a stone in a clear pool. Even rents are dropping in a few places. Housing is still an issue but is, perhaps, less impossible than it has been. Unions are striking and railroad workers are getting sick days. And in spite of the professional nay-sayers, the economy is not going to end up in a recession. Consumer confidence is up at least a bit.

The big drivers of change have lost some of their punch. COVID-19 continues but does not generate the headlines, nor the emotional response, it once did. COVID-19 is seen as pretty much in the rearview mirror. Florida county Republicans have declared that vaccines are bioweapons, but outside of Florida, few seem to care. Tucker Carlson has approached a pair of oligarchs to finance a comeback, but at this point, his program seems to have lost over 80% of his audience.[8] The Lying-for-dollars business plan overlooked the cost of defamation. The macabre death throes of Twitter speak for themselves.

What all this means is that of the original list, two major drivers of change are still operating at full force, White Supremacy / Christian Nationalism, and Climate Change. Both are still important and dangerous, but the other drivers are becoming less so. Tucker Carlson and others are being reduced to background noise equivalent to a short loop of elevator music. We no longer have the mutual causal links nor the synergistic impacts of multiple drivers feeding off each other the way in-your-face tech and lying for dollars did when joined with the dislocations of COVID-19.

All this good news is wonderful, but pales in comparison to the crucial news that should be written in the sky and shouted from the rooftops for all the willfully blind and deaf to see and hear. The good news is that a stake has finally been driven through the vampire heart of Trickle-Down Economics. The Inflation Reduction Act, The CHIPS and Science Act, the Bipartisan Infrastructure Deal all describe an economy in which "we all will do better when we all do well. It's time to build our economy from the bottom up and from the middle out."[9]

Did you hear that? A man too centrist, too middle-of-the-road, too institutional, with one stroke, broke with an economy based on "greed is good," an economy that stunted the nation as it fed the rise of the oligarchs, and was an important cornerstone of the dominant white male paradigm as it devolved into an ideology. Suddenly, there is an alternative paradigm providing an umbrella for the development of many new, rediscovered, more limited paradigms about social structures, programs, and objectives. This new alternative will rapidly gain ground. After all, Republican politicians who fought tooth and nail against this new paradigm are busy publicly claiming credit for the benefits.

The good news is that some millennials and most of the older Gen Z are already there. The inherent diversity of Gen Z culturally, racially, economically, experientially, and gender-identity-wise, when combined with their urban levels of connectivity, has exposed them to a greater diversity of daily-use paradigms than any previous generation. Because they grew up connected, for them the World is seen as flat, a network rather than a hierarchy. Because they grew up almost immediately connected to people, issues, sources, solutions, and stories from around the World, they have at their fingertips more potential answers than anybody has ever had before.

However, precisely because they must continuously learn and relearn the lessons afforded by misfeasance and malfeasance on the network, they are pragmatic. They may not be totally immune, but they are certainly more resistant than the "olds" to the stupidities spouted by a Carlson. This brings up a point that needs revisiting.

The benefits that Gen Z accrued from the in-your-face technology demonstrate that it is the connections between the technology and the lying for dollars business plan that are negative. The technology remains a driver of change, but it is neutral. In the hands of the "olds" listening to Carlson *et al*, it's one thing, but in the hands of the young, it's another thing entirely.

The boundaries and differences between the oldest Gen Z's, the voters between 18 and about 23 and the youngest millennials are not huge. A great deal of research has been done on both the Millennials and the Gen Z's from just before COVID-19 to more recently. For this discussion, the takeaway is that the older Gen Z's and the younger Millennials share values across a range of social, political, and economic issues, with Gen Z simply amplifying many of them. Overall, members of Gen Z look similar to Millennials in their political preferences.[11]

There is no effort here to paint the Gen Z and Millennials as pure as the wind-driven snow. There are young white nationalist and white supremacists

> A question and an observation.
>
> Are there three generations, young Gen Z, the old Millennials, and an in-between called Zillennials?[10]
>
> As this is written, it seems that Gen Z women are trending liberal while males are trending more conservative[17].

in the military. There are collegians so focused on causing pain and difficulty that it makes your blood curdle. And there are young candidates for all levels of elected positions whose understanding of history, i.e., slavery, staggers the imagination. However, at this moment, they seem a minority caught in a rip tide.

The point to be made here is there is a large group of voters with shared, or largely overlapping, values for whom the white, male, dominant cultural ideology fails to provide answers. Why do we care? Because when it is all about controlling my identity, my body, my future, and my life, or it is all about somebody I know, like, or love, it suddenly becomes more important, worth acting on.

Gen Z and the Millennials are changing state level political profiles by voting. College towns tend to grow and tend to be young and, these days, tend to vote. For example, Dane County Wisconsin has always been progressive. It contains Madison and the University of Wisconsin. In a recent election for a State Supreme Court Justice, Dane County alone became so dominant that it overwhelmed the Milwaukee suburbs and the more conservative rest of the State. "In effect, Dane has become a Republican-killing Death Star."[12] The under-30 vote has become a crucial demographic nationally and in local races, especially in recent midterms and specials.[13] Their perspective is that they have been abandoned by the Republicans.[14]

All of this provides a crucially important context for generating opportunities for Thrivancy Education. The crisis that has

> If the Republicans were to win all three in 2024, our whole effort getting this far will have been an exercise in futility.

been unfolding since 2008 might have achieved a tipping point at the 2024 elections. If Trump were to win the presidency, the changes he has stipulated and has promulgated in the past would derail the functioning of the Federal government and would reverberate globally. If the remnant Republicans, i.e., full-on Trump supporters, were to win the Senate, the House, and the Presidency, based on their stated goals, the American Idea would be effectively banished and the lights of the city on the hill would be dimmed, if not extinguished.

That statement sounds shrill, but the remnant Republican politicians, candidates, think-tanks, and supporters have made no secret of wanting to cancel global treaties, invade neighboring countries, sunset Social Security, Medicare, SNAP and school food programs, along with instituting a massively regressive flat sales tax, and making voting a privilege rather than a right.

The list could go on for quite a bit longer, but the point is made. The results will be catastrophic and would trigger a real and present crisis, ramifying across the breadth and depth of the American Idea and culture. The battles between those who would implement the retrogressive, repressive program, and the resistors would consume time, energy, and community with the outcomes uncertain. It would be a crisis indeed.

A solid prediction here is difficult. Will Trump successfully navigate all the indictments? Does that question even matter? Would Trump run as a felon? Or will Candidate Trump either drop out, or, if he runs, lose both the popular and the Electoral College vote. Will Gen Z combine with the Millennials in general, and along with progressives of all ages to overwhelm the residual Trump vote? It seems less likely, but there is a possibility that regressive candidates will lose in a clean sweep.

If it is not a clean sweep and the Remnant Party gains one or two of the power centers, such that the Federal Government becomes ineffective and major decisions are left up to the states with a sullied court system as a referee, it seems that there are three possible immediate metaphorical futures for the American Idea. To wit:

The Titanic – The "best-ever," Ship-of-State just keeps on keeping on in the face of information about changing contexts and dangers. Just like the 1%, the captain cannot see the danger through the fog, does not hear or listen to the warnings and a minor bump in the night sinks the whole affair. Most died a miserable, often lonely, cold, death, kind of like COVID-19. What kind of bump? Perhaps something akin to 2008. A few made the life-boats but not many. Many drowned. With this metaphor, America and the American Idea simply sinks into mediocrity. No longer the city on the hill and no longer a beacon; just another large country run by international, scavenger oligarchs living on borrowed time in limited bubbles.

The Hindenburg – The Hindenburg was beautiful, cutting-edge, the biggest, the best, a source of pride and wonder; until it wasn't. A tiny spark, somewhere, nobody knows where exactly, brought the whole thing down in a cataclysm. Not everybody died, but there was no future, and little was left except ash. In America, where will the spark come from? Is it local? Is it generated overseas in a troll farm? Or is it somebody on Fox news such as a future Tucker Carlson making a buck being a hatriot? This metaphor suggests the unravelling of the American Idea is going to be quick, ugly, and unexpected, with not much left afterwards.

The Miracle on the Hudson – In January 2009, U.S. Airways flight 1549 with 155 people on board ran into a flock of birds, lost both engines, and had to land in the middle of the Hudson River. It was cold. The air temperature was 19*F and water temperature was about 41*F.

Through good luck, extraordinary skills, and the coordinated, rapid response of many individuals bringing to bear massive resources, nobody died. In this metaphor, there is no single attention riveting event that triggers a widescale response as the American Idea rapidly unravels. If you do not see the pattern, all the tiny little instances of unravelling are easily written off as unimportant, local, and just more of the same, until it isn't. When a large airliner lands at 140 mph in the middle of the river in a major city, it is a major event that disrupts the expected patterns. People suddenly start to pay attention.

The metaphor absolutely works because the relatively behemoth airliner ran into a couple of hundred pounds of birds, if that, and it went into total engine failure and started to fall out of the sky. If the plane is the sociocultural entity that is the United States, then the engines are the American Idea that has lifted it off the runway and given it altitude. Has it been a smooth climb? No. There has been slavery, internment, vigilantism, and a whole host of ugly ism's, but we were enroute to a different place.

Over the last half century, and especially in the last decade, the engines have swallowed lots of "birds" that have been getting larger and larger. It may have started with swallows, but with recent court rulings and legislation, we are up to geese. The engines have essentially lost power. We are on a glide path down. Let's hope and pray for a smooth landing. Let's hope nobody dies. And let's hope that enough people with the heavy-lifters rally around and the plane does not sink into oblivion.

Thrivancy Education clearly has a role in helping to prevent either the Titanic or the Hindenburg and once the plane is safely down, providing multiple escape and survival maps that keep the American Idea afloat. Strauss and Howe predicted, "People young and old will puzzle over what it felt like for their parents and grandparents, in a distantly remembered era, to have lived in a society that felt like one national community. They will yearn to recreate this, to put America back together again. But no one will know how."[2 p.276]

Thrivancy Education can help start to rebuild the national community by becoming an important part of building from the bottom up and the middle out. Thrivancy Education by its very structure and function becomes a foundational piece of a strong middle class that "is a prerequisite for robust entrepreneurship and innovation, a source of trust that greases social interactions and reduces transaction costs, a bastion of civic engagement that produces better governance, and a promoter of education and other long-term investments."[15]

To repeat some arguments already made earlier:

- A strong American middle class is a prerequisite for, and a product of, Resilience, and Resilience allows and supports the American Idea.

- Thrivancy Education exposes the individual to more paradigms, more paradigms support more choice, more choice supports more control, more control creates more confidence, and more confidence generates more investment in the future, including education.

- Thrivancy Education exposes students to a broader array of paradigms and provides the raw materials, ideas, and perspectives to support the individual's entrepreneurship and innovation.

- Thrivancy Education puts feet on the ground, both student and adult, to rebuild communications across broad swaths of society, increasing understanding of a broad range of paradigms leading to increased trust and easier, more confident social interactions.

- Thrivancy Education recruits a multitude of people, not just in the schools but across the villages, to build networks and connections leading to increased engagement by individuals and better governance.

- Thrivancy education builds networks and connections thereby increasing potential earning of social capital to underwrite the individual's innovation, intervention, and further investment across the whole village.

- Thrivancy Education, by its very nature, precludes the test-centric and the marshmallow schools thereby supporting the rebuilding of a national community.

- Thrivancy Education does one more thing that is crucially important for the survival of the American Idea. It stops the white male privatization of the paradigmatic or cultural commons. Metaphorically, and maybe not so metaphorically, the battle about "woke" has been a battle to drive every other paradigm from the cultural commons. With "woke, there is room for only one shared code, including a set of rules, definitions, assumptions, concepts, values, practices, and connections that allow one to assign meaning, or

> Republican legislatures are rescinding labor laws and protections for children, as young as 14. This is not Thrivancy Education. As children are injured and/or die, this will be recognized as the continued privatization of childhood and the educational commons.

not, to the constant flow of inputs, stimuli, and experiences. Experience, information, and existence outside of that code is nonexistent and meaningless.

- Thrivancy Education throws up a wall and yells, Stop! The commons shall remain a commons.

- And finally, Thrivancy Education incorporates and inherently creates support for the American Idea of equality, justice, freedom, and self-determination in students as they grow through the system. If the American idea takes root in the young, it is safe.

President Biden expressed it well when speaking of John McCain,

> Every other nation in the world has been founded on either a grouping by ethnicity, religion, background. We're the most unique nation in the world. We're founded on an idea — the only major nation in the world founded on an idea. An idea that we are all created equal,  — in the image of God, endowed by our Creator to be — to be able to be treated equally throughout our lives.
>
> We've never fully lived up to that idea, but we've never walked away from it. You see, John is one of those patriots who, when they die, their voices are never silent. They still speak to us. They tug at both our hearts and our conscience. And they pose the most profound questions: Who are we? What do we stand for? What do we believe? What will we be?[16]

Thrivancy Education combined with these questions would reverberate across the warp and woof of American Culture and in doing so would undo the damage that has dimmed the lights of the city upon a hill. The American Idea would start to flourish, and more, many more, Americans would thrive.

A thriving America is absolutely safe haven for the American Idea. The clouds will dissipate, and it will not rain in America. The crisis will be survived, by a stronger and a more authentic city on the hill, a beacon of what can be.

# References

## Chapter 1. INTRODUCTION

[1] William Strauss and Neil Howe, *The Fourth Turning: An American Prophecy*, (New York, Broadway Books, 1997).

[2] C. Hedges, "The Deadly Rule of the Oligarchs." *Truthdig: Expert Reporting, Current News, Provocative Columnists*, (February 12, 2018). https://www.truthdig.com/articles/deadly-rule-oligarchs/.

[3] D. Racioppi, "Editor's Note: How We Define an Election Denier," *Erie Times-News,* (October 4, 2022). https://www.goerie.com/story/news/politics/2022/10/04/editors-note-how-we-define-an-election-denier/67098079007/.

[4] Melissa De Witte, 2022. "What to Know about Gen Z," (Stanford News, January 3, 2022). https://news.stanford.edu/2022/01/03/know-gen-z/.

[5] Hannah Hartig, "Americans Broadly Negative about the State of the Nation, but Most See a Better Year Ahead," (Pew Research Center, January 25, 2022). https://www.pewresearch.org/short-reads/2022/01/25/americans-broadly-negative-about-the-state-of-the-nation-but-most-see-a-better-year-ahead/.

[6] Shahram Heshmat, "The 8 Key Elements of Resilience," Psychology Today, May 11, 2020. https://www.psychologytoday.com/us/blog/science-choice/202005/the-8-key-elements-Resilience.

[7] Neil Howe, *The Fourth Turning Is Here*, (New York, Simon & Schuster, 2023) 226.

[8] "The Education of a Libertarian," Cato Unbound, April 13, 2009, https://www.cato-unbound.org/2009/04/13/peter-thiel/education-libertarian/.

[9] Nate Sweitzer, Andy Kroll, Andrea Bernstein, Ilya Marritz, "We Don't Talk about Leonard: The Man behind the Right's Supreme Court Supermajority," *ProPublica*, October 11, 2023. https://www.propublica.org/article/we-dont-talk-about-leonard-leo-supreme-court-supermajority.

[10] ABC News, "10 Cases of Alleged Arizona Voter Intimidation Referred to DOJ," ABC News, n.d. https://abcnews.go.com/Politics/cases-alleged-arizona-voter-intimidation-referred-doj/story?id=92054635.

[11] Joseph Stromberg, "What Really Sparked the Hindenburg Disaster?" *Smithsonian. Smithsonian.com*, May 10, 2012. https://www.smithsonianmag.com/science-nature/what-really-sparked-the-hindenburg-disaster-85867521/.

[12] Kaleena Fraga, "The Inspiring Story of the Miracle on the Hudson — and the Heroism of Pilot Sully Sullenberger," *All That's Interesting*, January 11, 2024. https://allthatsinteresting.com/miracle-on-the-hudson.

[13] Jenna L. Clark, Sara B. Algoe, and Melanie C. Green, "Social Network Sites and Well-Being: The Role of Social Connection," *Current Directions in Psychological Science* 27, no.1 (2018): 32–37. https://doi.org/10.1177/0963721417730833.

[14] Leah Marone, "Resilience: The Power to Overcome, Adjust, and Persevere," *www.psychology today.com*, June 27, 2021. https://www.psychologytoday.com/us/blog/gaining-and-sustaining/202106/Resilience-the-power-overcome-adjust-and-persevere.

[15] Chris Taylor, "How to repair our shrinking social, job networks," *Reuters*, July 21, 2021 https://www.reuters.com/lifestyle/how-repair-our-shrinking-social-job-networks-2021-07-22/

[16] George Petras, "US Suicide Rate Reaches Highest Point in More than 80 Years: See What Latest Data Shows," *USA Today*, November 29, 2023. https://www.usatoday.com/story/graphics/2023/11/29/2022-suicide-rate-historical-chart-comparison-graphic/71737857007/.

[17] Richard Weissbourd, Milena Batanova, Virginia Lovison, and Eric Torres, "Loneliness in America: How the Pandemic Has Deepened an Epidemic of Loneliness and What We Can Do about It," *Making Caring Common*, February 2021. https://mcc.gse.harvard.edu/reports/loneliness-in-america.

## Chapter 2. HOW DID WE GET HERE?

[1] Alex Domash, "Americans Are Becoming Climate Migrants before Our Eyes," *The Guardian*, October 2, 2020, https://www.theguardian.com/commentisfree/2020/oct/02/climate-change-migration-us-wildfires.

[2] Columbia Climate School. "Megadrought in Southwest Is Now the Worst in at Least 1,200 Years, Study Confirms." *State of the Planet*, February 14, 2022. https://news.climate.columbia.edu/2022/02/14/megadrought-in-southwest-is-now-the-worst-in-at-least-1200-years-study-confirms/.

[3] Thomas Reydon, "Philosophy of Technology," *Internet Encyclopedia of Philosophy*, n.d. https://iep.utm.edu/technolo/.

[4] David Russell Schilling, "Knowledge Doubling Every 12 Months, Soon to Be Every 12 Hours," *Industry Tap*, April 19, 2013. https://www.industrytap.com/knowledge-doubling-every-12-months-soon-to-be-every-12-hours/3950.

[5] M. McLuhan, "Cybernation and Culture," in *The social impact of cybernetics ...: Selected papers presented at a symposium on the social impact of cybernetics held in Washington, D.C., in November 1964, under the joint sponsorship of Georgetown University, American University, and the George Washington University*, ed. Charles R. Dechert. (London, University of Notre Dame Press, 1966), 105.

[6] Dexter Chapin, *Master Teachers: Making a Difference on the Edge of Chaos*, (Lanham: Rowman & Littlefield Education, 2009), 50.

[7] J. Lash, "Educating for Change," *HuffPost*, December 3, 2014. https://www.huffpost.com/entry/educating-for-change_b_6257210.

[8] N. Krueger, "Preparing Students for Jobs That Don't Exist," *Iste.org* (blog), August 31, 2021, https://iste.org/blog/preparing-students-for-jobs-that-dont-exist.

[9] Robert Parry, "Reagan's 'Greed Is Good' Folly," *Consortium News*, October 5, 2011, accessed April 14, 2024, https://consortiumnews.com/2011/10/05/reagans-greed-is-good-folly/.

[10] Howard Thurman, *Jesus and the Disinherited*, (Boston: Beacon Press, 2022).

[11] Robert Reich, "America's Billionaire Class Is Funding Anti-Democratic Forces," *The Guardian*, May 23, 2022, https://www.theguardian.com/commentisfree/2022/may/23/americas-billionaire-class-is-funding-anti-democratic-forces.

[12] S. Schwartz, "Inside the 'Private and Confidential' Conservative Group That Promises to 'Crush Liberal Dominance.'" *New York Progressive Action Network*, March 15, 2023, https://nypan.org/about/news-and-updates/2023/3/15/inside-the-private-and-confidential-conservative-group-that-promises-to-crush-liberal-dominance.

[13] James Baldwin, *The Fire next Time. The Open Library*, (New York: Vintage International, 1993), 102, https://openlibrary.org/books/OL1743367M/The_fire_next_time.

[14] National Centers for Environmental Information (NCEI). "Calculating the Cost of Weather and Climate Disasters," April 22, 2022, https://www.ncei.noaa.gov/news/calculating-cost-weather-and-climate-disasters.

[15] Laura Santhanam, "COVID Helped Cause the Biggest Drop in U.S. Life Expectancy since WWII." *PBS NewsHour*, December 22, 2021, https://www.pbs.org/newshour/health/covid-helped-cause-the-biggest-drop-in-u-s-life-expectancy-since-wwii.

[16] Timothy Pratt, "Covid Has Left Thousands of US Children Orphans. Few States Are Addressing the Crisis," *The Guardian*, April 8, 2023, sec. World news. https://www.theguardian.com/world/2023/apr/08/covid-orphans-us.

[17] Pouya Hosseinzadeh, Mordali Zareipour, Esfandyar Baljani, and Monireh Rezaee Moradali, "Social Consequences of the COVID-19 Pandemic. A Systematic Review." *Investigación Y Educación En Enfermería* 40 no. 1 (March 30, 2022). https://doi.org/10.17533/udea.iee.v40n1e10.

[18] United States Regional Economic Analysis Project, "Southwest vs. United States - Population Trends Report over 1958-2022," 4, Accessed March 21, 2024, https://united-states.reaproject.org/analysis/comparative-trends-analysis/population/reports/960000/0/.

[19] Arizona Department of Water Resources, "Conservation," Accessed March 21, 2024, https://www.azwater.gov/conservation/agriculture.

[20] US EPA OAR, "Climate Change Impacts by Sector," www.epa.gov, December 28, 2015, https://www.epa.gov/climateimpacts/climate-change-impacts-sector.

[21] Jeff Vandermeer, "Florida's Environmental Failure Is a Warning Sign for the U.S." *Time*, July 12, 2023. https://time.com/6288683/florida-desantis-environment-climate-change/.

## Chapter 3. WHAT IS RESILIENCY

[1] Ian Millhiser, "It Was a Great Day in the Supreme Court for Anyone Who Wants to Bribe a Lawmaker," *Vox*, January 19, 2022. https://www.vox.com/2022/1/19/22891236/supreme-court-ted-cruz-bribery-fec-loan-repayment-brett-kavanaugh-amy-coney-barrett.

[2] Aimee Picchi, *Money Watch*, "It Now Takes up to 66 Weeks to Pay for 52 Weeks of Middle-Class Basics," February 27, 2020 12:09 PM EST, CBS News, www.cbsnews.com, / Money https://www.cbsnews.com/news/a-thriving-middle-class-life-requires-more-than-a-years-income/.

[3] D. Madland, "Growth and the Middle Class." *Democracy Journal*, March 4, 2011, https://democracyjournal.org/magazine/20/growth-and-the-middle-class/.

[4] Federal Office for Spatial Development. "1987: Brundtland Report," 1987, https://www.are.admin.ch/are/en/home/media/publications/sustainable-development/brundtland-report.html.

[5] Anonymous

[6] Marissa King, and Balazs Kovacs, "Research: We're Losing Touch with Our Networks." *Harvard Business Review*, February 12, 2021, https://hbr.org/2021/02/research-were-losing-touch-with-our-networks.

[7] Tom Flood, conversation with author, "Community Design," April 15, 2022.

[8] "IHeartMedia, Inc.," www.iheartmedia.com., accessed March 21, 2024, https://www.iheartmedia.com.

[9] D. Simpson, "Semiotics," condor.depaul.edu., accessed March 20, 2024, https://condor.depaul.edu/dsimpson/pers/semiotics.html.

[10] Gregory Bateson, "Steps to an Ecology of Mind Collected Essays in Anthropology, Psychiatry, Evolution, and Epistemology," (Northvale, Jason Aronson, 1972), https://ejcj.orfaleacenter.ucsb.edu/wp-content/uploads/2017/06/1972.-Gregory-Bateson-Steps-to-an-Ecology-of-Mind.pdf.

[11] Molly McElroy, "While in Womb, Babies Begin Learning Language from Their Mothers," *UW News*, 2019, https://www.washington.edu/news/2013/01/02/while-in-womb-babies-begin-learning-language-from-their-mothers/.

[12] Caroline Ratcliffe, and Emma Kalish. "Escaping Poverty," The Urban Institute, 2017, https://www.urban.org/sites/default/files/publication/90321/escaping-poverty.pdf.

[13] Isabel Sawhill, "Social Capital: Why We Need It and How We Can Create More of It," 2020, https://www.brookings.edu/wp-content/uploads/2020/07/Sawhill_Social-Capital_Final_07.16.2020.pdf.

[14] Gregory Bateson, *Mind and Nature: A Necessary Unity*. Cresskill, N.J.: Hampton Press, Inc, 1979.

## Chapter 4. PARADIGM DEVELOPMENT AND FUNCTION

[1] Eesha Pendharkar, "A $5 Million Fine for Classroom Discussions on Race? In Tennessee, This Is the New Reality," *Education Week*, August 3, 2021, https://www.edweek.org/leadership/a-5-million-fine-for-classroom-discussions-on-race-in-tennessee-this-is-the-new-reality/2021/08.

[2] Adam Liptak, and Nick Corasaniti, "Supreme Court to Hear Case on State Legislatures' Power over Elections," *The New York Times*, June 30, 2022, https://www.nytimes.com/2022/06/30/us/politics/state-legislatures-elections-supreme-court.html.

[3] W.S. Smith, "Aristotle and Our American Oligarchy," The Center for the Study of Statesmanship, Accessed March 21, 2024. https://css.cua.edu/ideas_and_commentary/aristotle-and-our-american-oligarchy/.

[4] Ibram X, Kendi, "There Is No Debate over Critical Race Theory." *The Atlantic*, July 9, 2021, https://www.theatlantic.com/ideas/archive/2021/07/opponents-critical-race-theory-are-arguing-themselves/619391/.

[5] Kevin Kruse, "Opinion, Critical Race Theorists Do Not Do What Ted Cruz Says They Do." *MSNBC.com*, June 20, 2021, https://www.msnbc.com/opinion/ted-cruz-s-erroneous-definition-critical-race-theory-explains-white-n1271484.

[6] Caitlin O'Kane, "Nearly a Dozen States Want to Ban Critical Race Theory in Schools," *www.cbsnews.com*, May 20, 2021, https://www.cbsnews.com/news/critical-race-theory-state-bans/.

[7] Eesha Pendharkar, "A $5 Million Fine for Classroom Discussions on Race? In Tennessee, This Is the New Reality." *Education Week*, August 3, 2021, https://www.edweek.org/leadership/a-5-million-fine-for-classroom-discussions-on-race-in-tennessee-this-is-the-new-reality/2021/08.

[8] J.L. Cook, "Wisconsin School Board Members Vote against Free Meal Program Because They Don't Want Families to 'Become Spoiled.'" *The Root*, August 28, 2021, https://www.theroot.com/wisconsin-school-board-members-vote-against-free-meal-p-1847577986.

[9] Lisa Sharon Harper, *Fortune: how race broke my family and the World -and how to repair it all*, (Brazos Press, Baker Publishing. 2022).

[10] Keri Leigh Merritt, *Masterless Men: poor whites and slavery in the antebellum south*, (Cambridge University Press, 2018).

[11] Fritjof Capra, & Ugo Mattei, *The Ecology of Law: toward a legal system in tune with nature and community.* (Oakland: Berrett-Koehler, 2015), 201.

[12] William Strauss, and Neil Howe, *The Fourth Turning: An American Prophecy.* (New York: Broadway Books, 1997)

## Chapter 5. HOW DO WE CHANGE PARADIGMS TO BUILD RESILIENCE?

[1] Thomas S. Kuhn, *The Structure of Scientific Revolutions*, (Chicago University Press, 1970).

[2] Richard J. Borden, "Gregory Bateson's Search for 'Patterns Which Connect' Ecology and Mind," *Human Ecology Review*, 23, no. 2 (December 13, 2017), 87–96. https://doi.org/10.22459/her.23.02.2017.09.

[3] Gregory Bateson, *Mind and Nature: A Necessary Unity*, (Cresskill, N.J.: Hampton Press, Inc, 1979).

[4] Dina G. Borzekowski, Mussa L. Chale, and Charlotte Cole. "Tanzania Pilot," *na2ure.org*. Accessed March 21, 2024. https://na2ure.org/prior-research/.

[5] na2ure.org., "Home.," Accessed March 21, 2024, https://na2ure.com/.

[6] Aldo Leopold, *A Sand County Almanac*, (Oxford University Press, 1968).

[7] Rachel Carson, *Silent Spring*. 1962. Reprint, (Mariner Books: Houghton Mifflins, 2002).

[8] James Lovelock, *Gaia: A New Look at Life on Earth*, (New York: Oxford University Press, 2000).

[9] Jack Guy, "Teenage Boy Goes Blind after Existing on Pringles and French Fries," CNN, September 3, 2019, https://www.cnn.com/2019/09/03/health/poor-diet-blindness-scli-intl/index.html.

[10] Ludwig Von Bertalanffy, *General System Theory: Foundations, Development, Applications*, (New York: Braziller, 1968).

[11] William Ross Ashby, *Introduction to Cybernetics*, (S.L.: Franklin Classics, 2018).

[12] Robert C. Barkman, "See the World through Patterns | Psychology Today," www.psychology today.com, January 18, 2018, https://www.psychologytoday.com/us/blog/singular-perspective/201801/see-the-world-through-patterns.

[13] Augustus De Morgan, Sophia Elizabeth De Morgan, and University of California Libraries, *A Budget of Paradoxes. Internet Archive.* (London: Longmans, Green, and Co., 1872), https://archive.org/details/budgetofparadoxe00demorich.

[14] Seymour Epstein, (2010). Demystifying Intuition: What It Is, What It Does, and How It Does It, *Psychological Inquiry* 22, 4, 295-312, https://doi.org/10.1080/1047840X.2010.523 875.

[15] Tom Perkins, "Half of Recent US Inflation due to High Corporate Profits, Report Finds," *The Guardian*, January 19, 2024, sec. Business. https://www.theguardian.com/business/2024/jan/19/us-inflation-caused-by-corporate-profits.

[16] Fritjof Capra, and Ugo Mattei, U. *The ecology of law: toward a legal system in tune with nature and community*, (Oakland: Berrett-Koehler, 2015).

[17] Jay W. Forrester, *Urban Dynamics*, 1969, Reprint, (Albany, New York: System Dynamics Society, 2015).

## Chapter 6. THE RESILIENCY PARADIGM AND THRIVANCY EDUCATION

[1] Monticello, "Preparing for the Expedition," 2019, https://www.monticello.org/thomas-jefferson/louisiana-lewis-clark/preparing-for-the-expedition/.

[2] Nur Ibrahim, "Did Trump Say Election Fraud Allows for 'Termination' of US Constitution?" Snopes, December 5, 2022, https://www.snopes.com/fact-check/trump-termination-us-constitution/.

[3] Paige Bennett, "Climate-Related Damage Costs $16 Million per Hour on Average Globally - PopularResistance.org," PopularResistance.org, October 10, 2023, https://popularresistance.org/climate-related-damage-costs-16-million-per-hour-on-average-globally/.

[4] Jason Wilson, "'Red Caesarism' Is Rightwing Code – and Some Republicans Are Listening." *The Guardian*, October 1, 2023, sec. World news, https://www.theguardian.com/world/2023/oct/01/red-caesar-authoritarianism-republicans-extreme-right.

[5] eleducation, "Who We Are," https://eleducation.org/who-we-are, accessed April 16, 2024.

[6] Robert Fulghum, *All I Really Need to Know I Learned in Kindergarten*, (Fawcett, 1993).

[7] California Department of Education, "Kindergarten Frequently Asked Questions," (California Department of Education)," accessed March 21, 2024, https://www.cde.ca.gov/ci/gs/em/kindergartenfaq.asp.

[8] Elizabeth Ainslie, "NYC Kindergarten Admissions in the Age of COVID-19," Parents League of New York, June 25, 2021, https://www.parentsleague.org/blog/te-assessment-nyc-kindergarten-admissions.

[9] "Texas Legislators Approve Bill to Allow School Districts to Replace Counselors with Chaplains," Texarkana Gazette, May 24, 2023. https://www.texarkanagazette.com/news/2023/may/24/texas-legislators-approve-bill-to-allow-school/.

[10] Kathleen Dean Moore, *Great Tide Rising*, (Counterpoint, 2016) 318.

[11] William Strauss, and Neil Howe, *The Fourth Turning: An American Prophecy*, (New York: Broadway Books, 1997).

[12] eleducation.org., "EL Education," accessed March 22, 2024. https://eleducation.org/resources/reopening-guidance-a-transformative-opportunity-for-more-equitable-schools.

[13] Edutopia, "Integrated Studies," George Lucas Educational Foundation, accessed February 12, 2024, https://www.edutopia.org/integrated-studies.

[14] Shelby LeQuire, "The History of Women as Teachers," The Western Carolina Journalist, May 4, 2016, https://thewesterncarolinajournalist.com/2016/05/04/the-history-of-women-as-teachers/.

[15] "Defining Critical Thinking," Foundation for Critical Thinking, 2019, accessed March 21 2024, https://www.criticalthinking.org/pages/defining-critical-thinking/766.

[16] "The Four Elements of Humane Education," Institute for Humane Education, accessed March 22, 2024, https://humaneeducation.org/the-four-elements-of-humane-education/.

[17] J. Sumner, "Education and the Civil Commons," in *Educational Commons in Theory and Practice*, eds, A.J. Means, D.R. Ford, G.B. Slater, (New York. Palgrave Macmillan 2017), https://doi.org/10.1057/978-1-137-58641-4_11

[18] Valerie Strauss, "Privatization of Public Education Gaining Ground, Report Says," *Washington Post*, April 18, 2022. https://www.washingtonpost.com/education/2022/04/18/privatization-of-public-education-gaining-ground/.

[19] "Entry Level Programmer Salary in the United States," Salary.com, 2021, accessed April 16, 2024, https://www.salary.com/research/salary/posting/entry-level-programmer-salary.

## Chapter 7. THRIVANCY EDUCATION MANAGEMENT

[1] nces.ed.gov., "Program for International Student Assessment (PISA) - Welcome to PISA 2018 Results," 2018, accessed March 25, 2024, https://nces.ed.gov/surveys/pisa/pisa2018/index.asp#/.

[2] Dana Goldstein, "'It Just Isn't Working': PISA Test Scores Cast Doubt on U.S. Education Efforts," *The New York Times*, December 3, 2019. https://www.nytimes.com/2019/12/03/us/us-students-international-test-scores.html.

[3] Dana Goldstein, "The PISA Puzzle." *Slate*, December 3, 2013, https://slate.com/human-interest/2013/12/pisa-results-american-kids-did-not-do-well.html.

[4] Martin Carnoy, and Richard Rothstein, "'PISA Day'—an Ideological and Hyperventilated Exercise," Economic Policy Institute, (blog), December 1, 2013, https://www.epi.org/blog/pisa-day-ideological-hyperventilated-exercise/.

[5] F. Heylighen, and C. Joslyn, "The Law of Requisite Variety," *Principia Cybernetica Web*, Aug 31, 2001, accessed March 16, 2024, http://pespmc1.vub.ac.be/REQVAR.html.

[6] M.F. Smith, "Evaluability Assessment," *Encyclopedia of Evaluation*, 2005, https://doi.org/10.4135/9781412950558.n177.

[7] Laura Boyce, "Laura Boyce: Kids on the Supposed 'McDonald's Track' Are Living in a Rigged System," Network For Public Education, January 19, 2022, https://networkforpubliceducation.org/blog-content/laura-boyce-kids-on-the-supposed-mcdonalds-track-are-living-in-a-rigged-system/.

[8] Stafford Beer, *Diagnosing the System: For Organizations.* (Chichester: J. Wiley, 1985).

[9] Patrick Hoverstadt, *The Fractal Organization*, (John Wiley & Sons, 2011).

[10] Russell L. Ackoff, "*A brief guide to interactive planning and idealized design*," (Linkoping University, 2001), https://www.ida.liu.se/~steho87/und/htdd01/AckoffGuidetoIdealized Redesign.pdf

## Chapter 8. CAN THE AMERICAN IDEA SURVIVE?

[1] Samantha Fields, "How the World's Richest People Became Much Richer during the Pandemic," *Marketplace*, January 16, 2023, https://www.marketplace.org/2023/01/16/how -the-worlds-richest-people-became-much-richer-during-the-pandemic/

[2] William Strauss, and Neil Howe, *The Fourth Turning : An American Prophecy*, (New York: Broadway Books, 1997).

[3] Amanda Marcotte, "Tax Billionaires for Their Own Good," *Salon*, July 17, 2023. https://www. salon.com/2023/07/17/billionaires-arent-doing-great--for-their-mental-health-time-to -drastically-raise-their/.

[4] Matthew Desmond, "Why Poverty Persists in America," *The New York Times*, March 9, 2023, sec. Magazine. https://www.nytimes.com/2023/03/09/magazine/poverty-by- america-matthew-desmond.html.

[5] Nick Hanauer, and David Rolf. "The Top 1% of Americans Have Taken $50 Trillion from the Bottom 90%—and That's Made the U.S. Less Secure," *Time*, September 14, 2020, https://time.com/5888024/50-trillion-income-inequality-america/.

[6] Elie Mystal, "The Stench of Corruption Is Growing Stronger around the Supreme Court," *The Nation*, November 22, 2022, https://www.thenation.com/article/politics/the- stench-of-corruption-is-growing-stronger-around-the-supreme-court/.

[7] Keith Humphreys, "Young People Are Committing Much Less Crime. Older People Are Still Behaving as Badly as Before," *Washington Post*, September 7, 2016, https://www. washingtonpost.com/news/wonk/wp/2016/09/07/young-people-are-committing-much- less-crime-older-people-are-still-behaving-as-badly-as-before/.

[8] Mabinty Quarshie, "Will Tucker Carlson Be a Kingmaker in the 2024 Race?," *Washington Examiner*, July 15, 2023. https://www.washingtonexaminer.com/news/campaigns/tucker -carlson-kingmaker-2024-gop.

[9] Nick Hanauer, and Eric Beinhocker, "'Middle-Out': More than a Slogan," *Democracy Journal*, April 9, 2021, https://democracyjournal.org/arguments/middle-out-more- than-a-slogan/.

[10] Justin Charity, "It's Time to Accept That Millennials and Gen Z Are the Same Generation," *The Ringer*, December 31, 2021, https://www.theringer.com/year-in-review/2021/12/31/ 22860610/millennials-zoomers-gen-z-same-generation-olivia-rodrigo.

[11] Kim Parker, and Ruth Igielnik, "On the Cusp of Adulthood and Facing an Uncertain Future: What We Know about Gen Z so Far," Pew Research Center, May 14, 2020, https://www.pew research.org/social-trends/2020/05/14/on-the-cusp-of-adulthood-and-facing-an-uncertain -future-what-we-know-about-gen-z-so-far-2/.

[12] Charlie Mahtesian, and Madi Alexander, "'This Is a Really Big Deal': How College Towns Are Decimating the GOP," *Politico*, July 21, 2023, https://www.politico.com/news/magazine/2023 /07/21/gop-college-towns-00106974.

[13] Celinda Lake, and Mac Heller, "2024 Won't Be a Trump-Biden Replay. You Can Thank Gen Z for That," *Washington Post*, July 19, 2023, https://www.washingtonpost.com/opinions/2023/07/19/gen-z-voters-2024/.

[14] Rodge Reschini, "GOP Isn't Interested in Gen Z," *USA Today*, July 10, 2023, https://www.usatoday.com/story/opinion/2023/07/10/republicans-alienate-gen-z-voters-inflation-housing-family-values/70389574007/.

[15] D. Madland, "Growth and the Middle Class," *Democracy Journal*, March 4, 2011, https://democracyjournal.org/magazine/20/growth-and-the-middle-class/.

[16] The White House, "Remarks by President Biden Honoring the Legacy of Senator John McCain and the Work We Must Do Together to Strengthen Our Democracy," The White House, September 29, 2023, https://www.whitehouse.gov/briefing-room/speeches-remarks/2023/09/28/remarks-by-president-biden-honoring-the-legacy-of-senator-john-mccain-and-the-work-we-must-do-together-to-strengthen-our-democracy/.

[17] John Burn-Murdoch, "A New Global Gender Divide Is Emerging," *Financial Times*, January 26, 2024, https://www.ft.com/content/29fd9b5c-2f35-41bf-9d4c-994db4e12998.

# Index

www.ingramcontent.com/pod-product-compliance
Lightning Source LLC
Chambersburg PA
CBHW062035270326
41929CB00014B/2437